I ALMOST KILLED GEORGE BURNS!

AND OTHER GUT-SPLITTING TALES FROM THE WORLD'S GREATEST COMEDY EVENT

I ALMOST KILLED GEORGE BURNS!

AND OTHER GUT-SPLITTING TALES FROM THE WORLD'S GREATEST COMEDY EVENT

ANDY NULMAN

ECW PRESS

The publication of *I Almost Killed George Burns!* has been generously supported by The Canada Council, the Ontario Arts Council, and the Government of Canada through the Book Publishing Industry Development Program.

CANADIAN CATALOGUING IN PUBLICATION DATA
Nulman, Andy
I almost killed George Burns!: and other gut-splitting tales
from the world's greatest comedy event
ISBN 1-55022-464-6
1. Comedians – Anecdotes. 2. Montréal Just for Laughs Festival – Anecdotes.
3. Stand-up comedy – Anecdotes. I. Title.
PN1969.C65N84 2001   792.7'028'0922   C2001-930734-9

Back cover photo from Just For Laughs archives.
Author photo by Laurence Labat.
Interior photos courtesy Just For Laughs archives.
Cover and interior design by Guylaine Régimbald – SOLO DESIGN.
Copyediting by Mary Williams.
Typesetting by Yolande Martel.
This book is set in The Sans and Alexander.

Printed by Transcontinental.
Distributed in Canada by General Distribution Services,
325 Humber College Boulevard, Etobicoke, Ontario M9W 7C3.
Distributed in the United States by LPC Group,
1436 West Randolph Street, Chicago, IL 60607, U.S.A.
Distributed in Europe by Turnaround Publisher Services, Unit 3,
Olympia Trading Estate, Coburg Road, Wood Green, London N2Z 6T2.
Distributed in Australia and New Zealand by Wakefield Press,
17 Rundle Street (BOX 2266), Kent Town, South Australia 5071.

Published by ECW PRESS
Suite 200
2120 Queen Street East
Toronto, Ontario M4E 1E2.

ecwpress.com

PRINTED AND BOUND IN CANADA

To Aidan Foster, The Sweet, and especially my Ski.

A C K N O W L E D G M E N T S

I had just turned nineteen years old when I met Timothy Leary. He was appearing in North American comedy clubs as part of what he called a "stand-up lecture tour," and I got to go backstage at Yuk Yuk's for some face time with this counterculture guru. With a copy of his book *The Intelligence Agents* tucked under my arm, I shyly approached to have it autographed. His stringy white hair shimmied as he scribbled a lengthy salutation in black marker. Standing by awkwardly, I tried to make small talk as he signed.

"What's the most important part of writing a book?" I inquired.

"That's easy," he replied. "Without a doubt, it's the acknowledgments page."

"Is that because it expresses your sincere appreciation to those who helped you get to be an author?" I asked naively.

"No," he smiled. "It's because every name you mention on it is one more person obliged to buy your book."

I never forgot those words of wisdom. So, with them in mind, let me express my sincerest thanks to . . .

- The Book Brigade: ECW publisher Robert Lecker, editor extraordinaire Mary Williams, the pavement-pounding Francesca LoDico, and Jennifer Lokash.
- My book agent, Robert Mackwood, who believed in this one long after most people told him to take a hike with it.
- My loving family: my dad, Norman; my late mom, Carol; my in-laws, Faigie and Seymour and Lou; my sister, Nancy; brothers-in-law Steven, Howard, Henry, Steven, and Gary; sisters-in-law

Gail, Joanne, and Paula; Uncle Barry and Nicole; cousins Lorne
and Alison; nieces Hailey, Laura, and Meg; nephews Gregory and
Justin.

- My brother, Stuart, for remembering the most arcane details, for
saving every piece of communication ever produced by Just For
Laughs, and for allowing me access to it without having to lay
down any collateral.

- My family at Just For Laughs: Bruce Hills, Willie Mercer, Jodi
Lieberman, Robin Altman, Maria Gastaldi, Pierre Girard, Alain
Cousineau, Marc Hamou, Brentmonster Schiess, the Rozon sis-
ters, and, most notably, the grand and glorious Gilbert Rozon.

- Everybody at Airborne Entertainment, particularly my longtime
faithful assistant, Diane Shatz, and my partner-cum-brother,
Garner Bornstein, the most generous man on earth.

- The Top-40 under 40 gang.

- My showbiz pals: Arthur Price, Don Rickles, George Schlatter,
George Christy, Tony O, George Anthony, Fred Nicolaidis, Ed
Robinson, Ivan Fecan, Howard Lapides, Bill Brownstein, Rubin
Fogel, and Howard Busgang.

- Everybody who's now pissed off that I forgot them.

- Last, but not least, all those who laughed with—and not at—
me.

C O N T E N T S

F O R E W O R D

Hello Andy.

Here I am talking about your book, which I don't plan to read. Let's call this foreword what it really is—a mercy favor.

It was a real pleasure to be in Montreal at your Comedy Festival, of which I must say the money wasn't too great and your personality didn't warm it up any for me. The only exciting thing was that I saw a couple of Montreal Canadiens playing hockey on the street.

You are indeed a big promoter. Let's have lunch some day. Don't count on it, but I like to say that so you'll feel good. So, what else can I say, except that knowing you has been not a real treat . . . but, hey, let's go along with it.

Good luck with this book. If people read it, they are definitely lonely. Take care, and if the book sells big, you'll be a personal friend. If it doesn't, please don't call.

—Don Rickles

FOREWORD

The toughest thing to write is a book about comedy. The only thing more difficult than that is to write about a man who wrote a book about comedy. The only thing even more difficult is to write a foreword about a man who wrote a book about comedy and in that book told you everything there is to know about himself. Such a man is Andy Nulman, and such a book is *I Almost Killed George Burns*! The title of the book does not make it any easier to write a warm and fuzzy article about someone who would admit to such an act.

If you ever met Andy Nulman, you would most certainly remember him forever. People might say he has a Napoleon complex, except Napoleon was much too shy and gentle for any such comparison. Andy is a double type A, a whirlwind, a dynamic force field of energy, joy, and creativity. Andy is slightly under six feet tall, if you call nine inches a slight difference. But, let's face it, nine inches is only a slight difference to Milton Berle.

I must admit that I read Andy's book and enjoyed it, cover to cover. Now I'm going to read the inside. It is honest, true, funny, and very revealing about everyone, including Andy himself. He created, coordinated, and produced a truly magnificent collection of comedy and comedians at Just For Laughs, and this book accurately reflects some wonderful and lovely moments involving some wonderful and lovely people. Andy indeed qualifies for all of the above.

I thoroughly enjoyed reading this book, just as I have thoroughly enjoyed knowing Andy, who is what they call "a real piece of work." He is a one-man dynamic duo. I am sure that Just For Laughs will go on for many years, even though Andy is no longer running it. However, I doubt that it will ever be as much fun, as crazy, as outrageous, and as bizarre as it was when Andy was in charge. Read the book.

This is a really good book and fun to read. You can pick it up anytime. Putting it down is not easy, but then Andy does not deserve any put-downs.

He is a good friend. He is a good guy, and this is a good book. I would say many more wonderful things about Andy, but I'm not being paid that much . . . and almost everything wonderful I could say about Andy he has already said about himself. Modest he is not, but then I can find no reason under the sun for Andy to be modest about anything. As they say in Montreal, "va te faire foutre," which Andy has translated to me as meaning, "I am your friend forever."

—George Schlatter

ASK THE CEO

David Hyde Pierce was late. It wasn't his fault, though. The suave, eloquent costar of the sitcom *Frasier* was being stuffed into a costume for the all-important opening number of the even more all-important Just For Laughs Saturday night gala. Although there were ten other acts on the bill, David was the show's host, which meant that people had bought the festival's most expensive tickets primarily to see him. David's opening number was a crucial factor in setting the stage for the evening's ultimate success or failure, and this costume was a crucial factor in David's opening number.

Despite its importance, the costume didn't look like much—a nondescript suit-and-tie outfit—but it served to conceal David's more fashionable ensemble of supple black leather pants and raw silk sweater. The "suit" was actually a shell sewn together and cut into two halves, left and right, made to be torn off by a pair of barely clad dancers as David morphed from his stereotypical, erudite TV persona into a swivel-hipped songster.

We always pulled out all stops for the Saturday night gala host's opening number. Previous years' highlights included Lily Tomlin's resurrection of Ernestine, complete with 1940s switchboard; Kelsey Grammer and Brett Butler's O.J. Simpson chase mockery, complete with white Ford Bronco; and Nathan Lane's "Wind Beneath My Wings" duet with a ten-foot cardboard cutout of Bette Midler—to name but a few. This time around, David's parody of the Ricky Martin megahit "Livin' La Vida Loca" was to be no exception. We hired a half-dozen male and female dancers, re-created the checkerboard set featured in Martin's groundbreaking video, and bagged Bruce Vilanch, Hollywood's hottest comedy scribe, to pen new lyrics.

The concept was simple. After delivering a brief, pedestrian monologue in front of a bland curtain, David was to claim credit for the recent popularity spike in Latin music. After David uttered the line, "I'd like you to meet some of my friends," the two dancers would emerge and rip off his suit. This would be the cue for the curtain to rise, revealing the flashy set and the festival's live band, which would already be blasting the opening chords to the song.

Another magic moment would be born.

Unfortunately, the moment was experiencing labor pains. It was ten minutes past the scheduled 7:30 P.M. start time, and the costume halves weren't aligning properly. A team of dressers and seamstresses was busy onstage attending to the doubly dressed David; they were resewing the pieces of Velcro that would allow the suit to move relatively normally for the monologue but still tear away with a slight tug. The dancers stood around in graceful poses. The band members watched from their perch above, nonplussed. David, ever the pro, waited silently, patiently, with a smile.

And where was I during this calamity? Standing backstage, calmly sucking back an Orange Julius V-51 energy smoothie. Jeez, after fifteen years at the helm of the world's largest comedy event, I'd been through every backstage nightmare imaginable—and many that were unimaginable, even by the most demented of minds. This costume catastrophe wasn't even registering on the pacing scale (a form of crisis-intensity measurement: the faster my pace and the greater the distance I cover, the worse the problem). But Manon Lacasse, the stage manager, was in a state of panic. The crowd, as the cliché goes, was getting restless. Despite everyone's best efforts, yet another Just For Laughs gala show was getting off to a late start. "Andy," Manon hyperventilated, "you've got to go out on stage and kill some time!"

This was not a function foreign to yours truly. Truth be told, I actually relished the opportunity; so much so that every year as CEO I sauntered onstage before a gala to issue a festival state-of-the-union speechette, thanking 2,300 or so people for their valued and continued patronage. But I had delivered those bons mots the night before, and about twenty percent of gala audiences cross over from night to night. Recycling yesterday's niceties would come across as insincere, at best. Christ, I had ten seconds to come up with a whole new act.

"Give me the red light when you're ready to start the show," I told Manon. I grabbed a wireless mike and a bar stool and cut between the curtains, equipped with a simple plan. "Good evening ladies and gentlemen," I said as I placed the stool at center stage. So strange—the bigger the crowd, the more comfortable I feel. Another weird Nulman trait. Research has proven that public speaking is Western man's greatest fear, followed by fear of flying, rats, and dentists. To me, speaking to a crowd is more natural than sleeping. So I sat down and relaxed.

"Last night I subjected the audience to my standard sermon," I started. "But tonight we're gonna do something different. Tonight we're gonna play a game called 'Ask the CEO.' You must have a few questions about what it's like running Just For Laughs. Perhaps you're curious about the private lives of your favorite comedy stars. Well, for the next few minutes, I'm here to spill the beans. Who wants to go first?"

As the first question was posed (something about how I met my partner, Gilbert Rozon), a seamstress applied the finishing touches to David Hyde Pierce. Out of pity, I suppose, the backstage brigade let me answer the question. "Anything else?" I asked, delighted with the polite round of applause that greeted my rather innocuous tale. The dancers had assumed their positions, the band was poised to play, David was on his mark, Manon had switched on the red "get off the stage" light . . . and I was still yapping.

Two more questions. Two better stories. Two improved responses. One euphoric Andy. One pissed off backstage crew. Witnesses swear that Manon flicked the warning light so rapidly that it looked like a strobe. Yet, oblivious to the crimson beacon, I carried on. Other witnesses swear that the band actually plucked a couple of notes to rouse me from my storytelling stupor, but I was not only blind and dumb—I was deaf, too.

"Next question?"

By now the dancers were haggard, strewn about the stage on their knees, butts, or backs. The band members were caged animals, chomping at the bit to get the show started. Luckily, David was constrained by his costume, or I think he would've crawled under the curtain and throttled me. While finishing up the legend of how I almost killed George Burns during his 1993 festival appearance, I felt the unceremonious plunk of a quarter thrown from stage right. Ouch. I got the hint. I also got a hell of an ovation as I left the stage with the words, "Enjoy David Hyde Pierce!"; the applause was a sonic salve that soothed the sting of the coin.

And as the opening jolts of the Ricky Martin tune blasted through the hall, as the dancers slithered, as the costume detached perfectly, and as David Hyde Pierce crisply vocalized Vilanch's skewed lyrics, I strode off into the backstage darkness, thinking, with a smile: "You know, one day I gotta write a book about all this stuff!"

O N E

MY
DEFORMATIVE
YEARS

A career in comedy requires a particular personality. Comedians traditionally grow up as rebellious class clowns, learning to torture their teachers and entertain their schoolmates in one fell swoop. I, on the other hand, possessed a different attitude and skill set in school. While too affected to actually laugh at his sophomoric shtick, I would sit at the back of the room watching the class clown and think, "Hmm, if I could get this guy into a different school every week . . ."

I never wanted to be a comedian myself, but I always had the most profound respect for the profession. As the entertainment editor of Montreal's *Sunday Express*, I used to cover people like Jim Carrey, Howie Mandel, Andy Kaufman, Bob Saget, and *Welcome Back Kotter*'s Gabe Kaplan as they came through town. In my reverence for what they did, I actually tried my hand at stand-up comedy.

Once.

Because of my small-c celebrity status as a newspaper columnist, I was invited to be special guest host one Saturday night in 1981 at Yuk Yuk's Komedy Kabaret (dig that wacky spelling!).[1] The guest-host spot was a new concept the club was trying out, and I was honored to be

---

[1] Headlining that night was Carol Leiffer, the comic who was the inspiration for the Elaine character in *Seinfeld*. When I booked her for Just For Laughs in 1987, she asked me, "Weren't you that bad host in Montreal?"

the first. I was also humiliated by being the last. To say that I bombed is not only an understatement, but it's also a slap in the face to anyone who has ever died on a comedy stage before me or since. I was so damned awful that I literally considered killing myself that night. (Ever the pro, I had to interview *Private Benjamin* costar Eileen Brennan the next afternoon, so the suicide was put off until after the meeting. Thanks to Brennan's mothering, I live to tell this tale.)

So the class clowns went on to their graduate school without me in their midst. Still, the personality needed to run the Just For Laughs comedy festival has its own particular requirements. To succeed in this profession, one has to blend a pervasive sense of humor and a peculiar audacity with distinctive work-related experiences. The following three real-life adventures are the defining moments that helped shape me into the twisted character who would eventually spearhead the world's largest comedy event. Please don't hold them against me.

THE LUXOR STAKES

From the age of thirteen, I spent my summers working at some pretty crummy jobs. It could've been worse, I guess, but since most of my ex-tended family was involved in the schmatte business ("needle trade" for you non-Yiddish speakers), I at least had my pick of sweatbox facto-ries where I could labor as a minimum-wage slave.

Ah, the fond memories! There was Lori-Ann Dress, where the owner's dad would whack me on the kidneys with a cardboard tube. There was Lovable Knits, where the oppressive summer heat was augmented by hellish gusts from the steam press I operated from 8:00 A.M. to 5:00 P.M., Monday to Friday. But there was no place like Luxor Novelty, a plastics workshop owned by my cousin Isidore Socaransky. A glutton for pun-ishment, I worked there for two whole summers. Luxor didn't actually make plastics, but it silk-screened, cut, and sewed rolls of the stuff into tote bags, makeup pouches, and brush holders for companies like Avon. I still wake up in a cold sweat from nightmares of Luxor's finger-munching hot-stamping machine (yes, it was as evil as it sounds); I'm still amazed that I escaped from the place with all my digits.

The people who labored in this wood-floored danger zone were so diverse and outlandish that they could have been the cast of the next generation of *Star Trek*. They came from all over: Italy, Israel, Portugal, Germany, Spain, the Bahamas, rural Quebec. Each one was a unique character in his or her own right, which stoked the flames of the scheme I would soon hatch.

I arrived at Luxor during a tumultuous period in my young life. I was sixteen years old, liberated by my driver's license, filled with the piss and vinegar that comes with the coming of age. While still a kid, I was also a veteran of the backrooms, hardened by three years of factory experience. All of this, combined with the dramatis personae surrounding me, led to the creation of one of the great innovations of the industrial revolution: the Luxor Stakes.

For those of you who have never worked on a factory floor, it's important to understand its strict regimentation of time. A bell rings at 8:00 A.M. to signify the dawn of the new work day. It rings at 10:15 A.M. to mark the start of the morning coffee break and again, fifteen minutes later, to mark its finish. Same thing at noon and 12:30 P.M. for lunch, at 3:15 and 3:30 P.M. for afternoon coffee break; and, finally, at 5:00 P.M. for what we called "the Flintstone whistle," the much-anticipated quitting-time signal.

Day in, day out, the bells rang. Work stopped and started on cue. But after a few weeks of this Pavlovian monotony, I noticed something off-kilter. Every Friday afternoon, from 3:30 to 5:00, the women on the packing table and sewing machines didn't actually go back to work. Instead, they killed ninety minutes following each other to the bathroom. Two went, one returned; two more went, two returned, and so on and so forth. What they did in there remains a mystery, but the piles of cigarette butts and gossip tabloids strewn about in the vicinity of the bathroom provided enough clues for even the most amateur Sherlock Holmes.

It wasn't exactly a rage against the machine. This act of defiance was carried out daintily and with great tact. For years it escaped detection by Horst, the crusty foreman, and Johnny, his cologne-drenched lothario of an assistant. But, in the summer of '76, it caught the eye of this little shit disturber. Working in factories had given me much admiration for those who toil in them. It may have been a tough July and August for me, but I would return to my middle-class home at night and to school in the fall. These guys and gals were lifers. Needless to say, I wasn't going to rat them out. But my sixteen-year-old mentality wouldn't let me ignore the situation, either. The Luxor Stakes was my compromise.

Here's how it worked. I nicknamed all the packing and sewing ladies and threw their names into my baseball cap. There was Little Bear, Crazy Alice, Marleny, Madame Carmen, Lily Lemon, Boozer #1, Boozer #2, The Cow, Stumpleg, and many more. Some of the backroom boys put in a buck and pulled out two names. Like a racetrack quinella, the guy to have both of his women go to the bathroom first would win the pot. On its debut Friday afternoon, the Luxor Stakes worked like a charm. My friend Yama Spodek took home ten dollars (about three hours' pay) and we were off to the races.

The concept was so successful that we decided to run the stakes again. This time we let a few more people in on the secret and upped the ante to five dollars each. As creator and chief organizer, I took a ten percent commission off the top. The pot blossomed to seventy-five bucks, and once again the Luxor Stakes were up and running. Despite the increased buzz among the bettors on the floor, the participants remained oblivious and continued their nonstop treks to the toilet.

By the third week we'd established odds. We kind of knew who went, when, and how often. Thus, Crazy Alice was a 3-2 favorite while the stoic Marleny was a 25-1 long shot. My cousin Isidore found out, and he actually joined in. Isidore was a happy-go-lucky guy—while he wasn't going to punish his loyal staff for squandering an hour-and-a-half per week, he wasn't going to miss out on the action, either. Isidore's quasi-condoning of the offtrack betting system that bore his corporate name allowed us, once again, to increase the stakes and the number of participants. By this time the pot had shot up to over two hundred dollars, with multiple bets and winners.

Unfortunately, it all went to my teenage head. I got cocky. When the 3:30 bell rang on this particular Friday, I played a tape of the Kentucky Derby bugle call on my portable cassette machine. The ladies looked around in bewilderment. They were even more puzzled by the reaction of every man on the factory floor and many in the offices that surrounded it. Each of their trips to the bathroom was met by muffled exclamations of "Alright!" or "Aw, shit!"

Then all hell broke loose. At about 4:40 Crazy Alice and Madame Carmen got up to go, at the same time, from opposite ends of the factory. So much money was riding on the outcome, and whoever got there first would determine the winner. The new, untrained guys, unable to display a lack of emotion like us old hands at the game, started to go berserk.

"Go! Hurry up!" about seven of them shrieked in unison. The two bathroom-bound ladies looked back, baffled.

"Don't stop! Just go! Come on!" came the cries. The ladies stared at each other.

"Run! Run!" the guys wailed.

Crazy Alice turned around and headed back to her sewing machine. This was just too screwy, even for her. Five guys immediately tore up their tickets in disgust. Madame Carmen, the most elegant of the packers (and at best an outside chance), continued on her way with pride. When the bathroom door shut behind her, the two winners went haywire. This was the best one yet!

The following week, as expected, the pot shot through the roof. From Monday morning to Friday lunch the only thing the guys talked about was the Luxor Stakes. Handicappers watched for limping or other telltale signs of distress among the ladies that would hamper a smooth bathroom run. We considered establishing official rules and franchising the concept to other companies in the area. Once again 3:30 rolled around, and the bugle call sounded.

But this time the ladies didn't move.

They sat at their tables and machines and stared in revulsion at the goofs with whom they worked. Madame Carmen got up and said something unintelligible in a garbled mixture of Spanish, French, and English, but the ferocity of her message came through loud and clear. Carmen's outburst inspired an amazing show of solidarity among her male coworkers. Italian. Portuguese. Spanish. Black. White. Young. Old. They were all one. And they all acted in unison, crying, "It wasn't me!" as they pointed their fingers at the teenage outsider in their midst. "It was him!"

Me at sixteen years old. From the drudgery of the factory floor
to the glamor of the media biz in one summer!
(Note the reporter's notepad in the breast pocket.)

I learned some valuable lessons that Friday afternoon. One was, "You can fool all the people, but not for longer than three weeks"; Abe Lincoln would've been proud. Another lesson was that "He who executes gets executed." Luckily, the ladies didn't hold a grudge for long, or the rest of my summer would've become even sweatier than it already was.

Perhaps the whole episode was best summarized by Lily Lemon, the massive Bahamian woman with the zillion-dollar laugh. "Boy," she said to me with a wide grin, "you is a motherfucker!"

TOE BLAKE'S CHEEKS

While I was at Luxor I answered an interesting want ad in the *Sunday Express*. The paper, a tabloid heavy on sports and crime coverage, was looking for someone to bolster its sports department during the upcoming Summer Olympic Games, and maybe beyond. I don't think they received too many responses, because I was given an immediate appointment, on a Thursday lunch hour at the *Express*'s Roy Street offices, only a few blocks away from the Luxor compound.

It was my first real job interview, and I boned up on all sorts of sports minutiae and statistics. But that's not how I got the position. During the five minutes of experience I gained working on my high school yearbook, I'd been exposed to a newspaper layout sheet, and, lo and behold, that's the first thing I noticed on sports editor Gary McCarthy's desk. Impressed that I actually knew about this most rudimentary building block, he hired me on the spot. I would work Saturdays from about 1:00 P.M. to 9:00 P.M. for fifty dollars. I was in heaven.

Until the end of my first Saturday, that is—9:00 P.M., my ass! I didn't finish until 2:00 in the morning. I postponed, and postponed, then finally canceled the movie date I had with a high school babe named Rhonda Friedman. Worse yet, the guys I was working with, moonlighting sportswriters from other newspapers, were, in my words, "cynical loser alcoholics." I wanted to quit, and I whined all this to my father, who'd gotten out of bed to pick me up at the subway station. "Well, if they're such losers, then you should be able to run the place in six months," he challenged me. "Good thing they're not much competition for a big shot like you."

With this in mind, I changed my plan of attack. As much as I enjoyed sports, I looked at working in the sports department as the Trojan horse for fulfilling my true intentions and first real love—rock music. On Tuesday I called Rosa Harris, the paper's entertainment editor, and asked if she'd be interested in an article I had written for my college paper. It was about Peter Frampton, and—how timely!—he was coming to town the following week. "Why not?" she said.

Why not? Well, for one thing, I had just graduated high school; I had never even been inside a college. But opportunity was knocking, so, with a few quotes I'd stolen from *Circus* magazine,[2] I sat down and composed my first-ever article. The *Express* published my Frampton story, and I suddenly became a cog in the star-making machinery behind the popular song. Record companies called, offering me interviews with their talent rosters. Donald K. Donald, the local concert promoter, put me on his comp ticket list, and soon I was attending every show in town. While I dropped off the sweet-sixteen circuit, I was enjoying a lifestyle well worth giving up my Saturday nights for. The rest of the summer unfolded like this: I would work at Luxor all week, take off an afternoon or two to interview acts like Loggins and Messina, Chris de Burgh, or Kiss, and work sports on Saturdays, interviewing amateur athletes and fetching french fries for the guys. The pattern continued, minus Luxor, when I finally started college in the fall.

Within a year I had replaced Rosa as entertainment editor and stopped running errands, but I kept my finger in the Saturday sports pie. Due to my "seniority," though, I graduated from covering curling and bowling to the big leagues: I was assigned to help cover the Montreal Canadiens during the playoffs. These were the days of the Habs dynasty, when superstars like Guy Lafleur, Frank Mahovlich, and Ken Dryden ruled. My gig was to back up veteran sportswriter Brodie Snyder. I would hit the visitors dressing room after the game, get a bunch of quotes from the players (not the easiest task, considering their diction and vocabulary), let Brodie take what he needed for his main story, and use the rest for my sidebar.

---

[2] My favorite rock and roll publication and, ironically one I would write for two years later.

For about a week in 1979, though, I got my own beat, covering the New York Rangers as they challenged the Canadiens for the Stanley Cup. I shadowed the cantankerous Phil Esposito and disgraced glamor boy Don Murdoch, one of the few players with hair longer than mine. The Canadiens won in five, and I was there for the thrill of victory as they took the Cup on home ice. Better still, being a member of the working press earned me the most coveted invite in town—to the Canadiens' victory party. Most twenty-year-old males I knew would surgically remove their left testicle with a cold, rusty butter knife just to sniff such an invitation, let alone attend the party. Yet there I was, at the venerable Queen Elizabeth Hotel on an early June night, hanging with the Habs.

Combine the camaraderie of sports with the elegance of a ball, and you have a Stanley Cup party. It was unadulterated, dressed-up joy. Men were hugging, slapping each other on the ass, clinking glasses, and posing for endless photos in the classic arm-over-shoulder embrace. There were so many revelers that the Queen E staff had to open the wall to a second ballroom; they scrambled to lay out extra tables and place settings to deal with the overflow. Everyone was there—not just the '78-'79 championship team, but also Hall of Fame members of the Habs alumni, looked upon in awe by all in attendance.

One such alumnus was Toe Blake, the renowned Habs goal scorer of the thirties and forties who went on to become the uncompromising coach of the Canadiens dynasties of the fifties and sixties. During my Saturday nights at the *Express*, I would sit around with my sports department cronies watching the Habs games on TV, waiting for the final score so that we could put the paper to bed. Inevitably, at least once per game, the camera would zoom in on Blake, at that point retired, surveying his old domain from his familiar Montreal Forum seat. While his eyes still had the same intensity, his features had softened, most notably his cheeks, which had taken on a dignified grandfatherly droop. One of the recurring jokes around the office was, "I wonder what it would be like to pinch those cheeks?"

And now, at last, at the prestigious Canadiens Stanley Cup celebration, I had a chance to find out.

Spotting Blake across the room vainly searching for a table, I got up from mine, told my colleagues, "I'm about to realize a dream," and made my way towards him. "Excuse me, Mr. Blake," I said bashfully. "Grmmpph," Blake harrumphed, looking over my shoulder for a place to sit. Instinct told me to go back whence I came, but I ignored it. There was no malice in my intent.

"Uh, you kind of remind me of my grandfather, and I see you on TV every week, and there's something I always wanted to do," I rambled.

"Yeah, what?"

The instinct to flee intensified, but for some reason I persisted. "Can I pinch your cheeks?"

"What?" said Blake in disbelief.

"Go!" bellowed my instinct. "Escape while there's still hope!" But, swallowing all my good judgment, I reiterated my request. "Can I pinch your cheeks?"

Stunned, Blake gazed at me as if he had caught a Bobby Hull slapshot square in the forehead. Time stopped for a second. Then he erupted like Vesuvius.

"What are you, some kind of fucking faggot?" he barked. Oops. Too late to run now.

"You insulted me!" he shrieked. "You insulted me!"

I backpedaled as I backed away, "Aw, look, I really didn't mean to insult you, Mr. Blake. I'm so, so sorry. Really, I didn't mean anything . . ." I tiptoed hastily back to my table.

"What happened?" asked Jim Vani, the *Express*'s editor-in-chief.

"Oh, nothing," I lied. "Just keep eating." And then came the nuclear explosion.

"I'll kill the fucking faggot!"

With that Blake flipped over a table, sending dishes, glasses, and silverware crashing to the floor. People—most notably those seated at said table—screamed in terror. The orchestra stopped playing midsong. To make matters worse, Blake was charging towards me like a Brahmin bull, fire in his eyes and murder on his mind. "What's going on?" Vani demanded. "Don't look up!" I said. "Just keep eating!"

Picture the scene: an attacking Hall of Famer; a silent, dumbfounded orchestra; about a thousand alarmed guests, all rubbernecking for a glimpse of what's going on; and, at the eye of the storm, one single table of ten people concentrating intently on their plates, eating quietly.

I owe my life to Ron Andrews, then the National Hockey League's chief statistician. From the corner of my eye I saw him move to block Blake's path. Before snapping my attention back to my salad, I caught sight of Andrews's back, with two hands flailing over his shoulders. "Let me at him!" Blake kept bellowing. "I'll kill the faggot!" Andrews ushered the hyperventilating Blake to the back of the ballroom to calm him down. Meanwhile, back at our table, I finally explained what had detonated the outburst.

"Are you nuts? Are you insane?" cried Bob Amesse, the *Express*'s sports editor at that point and my best buddy at the paper. "This is a guy who wouldn't let his players finish practice until they puked!" Yeah, Bobby, thanks for telling me now. It was obvious that I had to lie low and remain inconspicuous for the rest of the evening, but there weren't many places for a guy with shoulder-length hair, wearing a white suit, to hide. So, I did the next best thing—I stayed in my seat and wore my sunglasses. What a master of disguise!

About an hour later, when the party had returned to normal, I summoned up enough bravado to get up from my seat once more, this time to have my picture taken with two spectacular trophies, the Stanley Cup and my date, Heidi Stober.[3] Making my way over to the Cup corner, I saw Blake out in the hallway near the ballroom's rear entrance. I'll never forget the sight—he was sucking back oxygen from a St. John's Ambulance tank. Toe Blake was breathing easier. It took me until his death in 1995 to do the same.

MR. CHICKEN

I was fired from the *Sunday Express* in 1982. Jim Vani had been replaced by Duncan Weir as editor-in-chief. Part of Weir's new team was a sales manager named Michael Lawton, a Dabney Coleman look-alike and Satan act-alike. For numerous reasons, Lawton and I never got along.

---

[3] I mention Heidi by name for a reason. Jim Vani is dead. So's Toe. Bob Amesse is AWOL. Heidi's the one person who can corroborate the tale from my point of view. Because of its incredible nature, most people who hear this story don't believe it, or at least they believe that I'm exaggerating. To them, I simply say, "Call Heidi Stober."

Here's one reason: at a massive promotional dinner and cruise that I had put together ("promotion manager" had been added to my job description), Lawton thought it would be a good gag to cut my tie in half. Har-dee-har-har. My response, which I thought to be equally amusing, was to toss a glass of red wine at his white Lacoste sweater. Sorry, sucker, you don't screw with my clothes.

A few months later, however, Weir was out and Lawton was in. His first act—other than maybe to commission a life-size statue of him-self—was to boot my ass as far out of sight as possible. I had less than a year to finish up my business degree at McGill University, and I was unemployed for the first time since I was thirteen. My situation didn't improve much upon graduation. The only interview I managed to score through the on-campus recruiting service was with General Foods; the exec doing the screening dismissed me with two words: "Oh, no." The only other offer tendered to me was selling insurance for Prudential. No offense, guys—I love insurance, but only when I'm buying it.

Forced into entrepreneurship, I started my own marketing and promotion business, Mondumar (I know, what a putrid name). One of my main clients was promoter Rubin Fogel, a friend from my *Sunday Express* days. He awarded me the contract to do PR for his concerts, particularly his comedy series, which is how I first got to work with Jay Leno, Mike MacDonald, Norm MacDonald, and Steven Wright. Over drinks one night, Rubin mentioned that he would love to do a Howie Mandel date. What a coincidence—Howie was another buddy of mine from the *Express* days. While Howie was still a struggling comic, not only did I give him tons of ink, but my parents—who were in the schmatte business like the rest of my family—had also showered him and his wife, Terry, with samples from Santa Cruz and other hot labels whenever they came over.

I called Howie at home and put him in touch with Rubin. Ever the mensch, Rubin came to me with a proposition: I could do my usual PR on this show, or, since I'd brokered the deal, I could copromote it with him. Thanks to a ten-thousand-dollar interest-free loan from my cousin Kenny Goodman (yes, also in the schmatte business), I was able to take Rubin up on his offer. So, on June 8, 1984, I became a concert promoter.

The night of Mandel's show was a forerunner to the many nights

I'd be spending at the St. Denis Theater. Tickets sold out quickly, and, being new to the game, I wanted to watch the people filing into my event. Outside the venue's glass front doors I saw someone scalping tickets; a sign of success, I guess. But—wait a minute—that's no ordinary scalper . . . that's Howie's national tour promoter! I ran to Rubin and dragged him to the scene of the crime. Rubin, the straightest man in this crooked business, confronted the guy and brought the whole episode to Howie's attention after the show. That tour promoter was relieved of his duties before our eyes. "Hey, guys," said Howie, looking over at us. "Interested in picking up some dates?"

Suddenly, we were nationwide. Things went so well in Canada that when Howie decided to undertake his first major American tour in '85, we got the nod. One year after promoting my first show, I found myself going over star-studded guest lists at L.A.'s Universal Amphitheater and scrapping with the union heavies at Carnegie Hall.

Touring with Howie wasn't easy. We could only go out on weekends, due to Howie's commitments to *St. Elsewhere*, the superb NBC hospital drama in which he starred as Dr. Wayne Fiscus. For a period of twelve weeks we were a team of seven, and we established the following routine: Howie, manager Terry Danuser, Howie's friends and opening acts Lou Dinos[4] and Tommy G., would all leave from L.A.; Al and Steve Mandel, Howie's dad and brother, who handled his merchandising, would depart from Toronto; I would take off from Montreal. We would meet in a given city on a Friday afternoon for a show that night, head off the next day to another city for a Saturday night show, then return to our respective hometowns and real lives on Sunday.

Howie was, and still is, a consummate businessman. He understands money better than most investment bankers. Ever hear the expression, "Waste not, want not"? Well, although Howie doesn't waste, he most

---

[4] In addition to performing the onstage chore of warming up the crowd, Lou also provided most of the offstage laughs, usually as the butt of Howie's practical jokes. Once, he was told that he could fly in first class with Howie, but since the ticket was booked for Terry Mandel, Lou would have to travel as a woman, complete with wig, makeup, and high heels. He did it. Another time, in Cleveland, Lou was performing in front of the curtain. Unbeknownst to him, the section of the stage he occupied was on hydraulics and could be lowered into the orchestra pit at the touch of a switch. Lou finished his routine with only his eyes peeking out above ground level.

certainly continues to want. Here's what I mean: after two sold-out shows in St. Louis on the tour's opening night, he came running off-stage, drained and dripping with sweat. We all huddled around and tossed laurels: "Great show, Howie!" "Incredible!" "Wow, what a start!"

"Forget that," Howie said, grabbing a towel. "How many T-shirts did we sell?"

It was the first time that any of us had done anything like this at such a level, so we learned as we went along. As tour manager, I was responsible for everything right up until showtime: booking flights and limos, doing sound checks, even making preshow announcements. I was responsible for everything that had to happen after the show, too: settling with the local promoter, arranging after-hours entertainment, ordering wake-up calls for the next day.

One of the first lessons I learned on the road was that the star is treated differently. In St. Louis I booked everyone's hotel rooms under their own names. After being hounded all weekend by fans, Howie was rightfully pissed. "You can't use my real name," he chided. "You have to use an alias." I suggested that we use "W. Fiscus," the name of his *St. Elsewhere* character. "Naw, they'll get that in a second," Howie moaned. "Next week, make sure to think up something no one will figure out."

Come Tuesday, I'm alone in my office booking the rooms for Friday night in Kansas City. "Yes, that's Nulman, Dinos, Danuser, Tommy G.; then there's Mandel, Al, Mandel, Steve, and Mandel, Howie," I said, before realizing my mistake. "Oh, jeez, can I change the last one? You see, he's a star, and he doesn't want people hassling him . . ." The Hyatt agent replied, "I understand sir. What name would you like to use instead?" Christ! I was under the gun, and I had namer's block. I wracked my brain for a pseudonym, but to no avail. "Sir? Do you have the name yet?" I was drawing blanks. Think! Think! "Sir? I have other customers waiting. Why don't you call me back?" Desperate for something—anything—I settled for the lamest of inspirations. Looking down at the soggy chicken sandwich I was eating for lunch, I blurted, "I've got it! Book it under 'Mr. Chicken'!"

I was the first of the pack to arrive in Kansas City that Friday, and immediately after checking in, as I am wont to do, I went shopping. Not only did it help pass the time and feed my compulsive consumption habit, but it also gave me a chance to mix with the locals and maybe overhear some buzz about that night's show. No such luck in K.C., so, after fine-tooth combing the Hallmark Mall, I made my way back to the Hyatt. When I arrived there was quite a ruckus going on at the check-in desk. Hey, look, it's Howie and the guys!

Oh, shit, it's Howie and the guys. And they're not happy.

"We all have *our* rooms," said Steve, confronting me, "but there's nothing for Howie. The hotel's sold out and we can't even find him a room, never mind a suite!" The front desk manager was apologizing profusely. "I'm so sorry. I have an A. Mandel, and an S. Mandel, but no H. Mandel anywhere." My body temperature microwaved to magma level. Shamefaced, I spoke up. "Try 'Mr. Chicken.'" The manager clicked the keyboard, and, to his delight, the code was cracked. "Oh, here it is! In the executive suite!"

Howie stared at me. "Mr. Chicken?" I tried to rationalize, saying that he'd told me to come up with a better alias. "Yeah," Howie responded, "but tell me what the fuck it is next time!"

A few hours later, all was forgotten, thanks to another great performance and the arrival of tour sponsor Budweiser with crates of T-shirts and other free junk for the seven of us. But there was to be one final poultry-based episode before we bid adieu to K.C.

Famished after a long day of travel and bouncing around onstage, Howie retired to his suite and called room service for a late-night meal. "Fine, and that's under what name?" the order taker asked.

"Howie Mandel."

"I'm sorry, sir, but that's not who is registered in the room."

"Let me explain. You see, I'm booked under an alias, but the name is Mandel. Howie Mandel."

"I show a Steve Mandel and an Al Mandel, but no Howie Mandel, sir."

"What's the difference? It's a salad. Just send it up, will you?"

"Sir, unless you are the registered guest, I can't send anything up to your room."

Admitting defeat, Howie sighed and, through layers of humiliation, grumbled, "Alright. Mister fucking Chicken!"

"It'll be right up."

I didn't hear the end of it the next morning. At the airport I realized that I had booked Howie under the same fowl name in Cleveland, so I snuck away and called the hotel to change the pseudonym to something a little more innocuous. Thank God they could do it. The flight left Kansas City a little late, but we were just in time for the afternoon meal. I was starved.

"Will you be joining us for lunch, sir?" the flight attendant said pleasantly.

"Whatchya got?"

"I've run out of beef, but I do have plenty of chicken."

"Forget it," I said, burying my head in my pillow. "I'm not hungry anymore."

After the final tour weekend, in Chicago, where Howie recorded an HBO special at the old Bismarck Theater, Rubin and I sat down for a postmortem. I had made more money in twelve weeks than I had the entire previous year. I raised my glass and thanked Rubin for the opportunity. "Oh, I gave your name to someone," he remarked nonchalantly. "He has this comedy thing he wants to talk to you about. His name is Gilbert Rozon."

The rest, as they say, is history. And so is the next chapter.

T W O

THE EARLY
DAYS

For the past decade and a half, I always presumed that whomever I was speaking to knew about Just For Laughs. And I'm making this somewhat immodest presumption right here, too—I mean, if you knew diddly-squat about the festival, why would you buy this book in the first place? (Okay, aside from the appealing cover, the catchy title, and the hot author portrait lurking within.)

However, merely knowing that something does exist doesn't necessarily provide you with insight into why it does. Hence this chapter. Believe me, I don't want to bore you with a detailed, analytical history of one of the world's most popular cultural events, but putting Just For Laughs in its proper perspective renders the juicy stories and insider dirt that fill up the rest of these pages even juicier and dirtier.

So bear with me . . .

First of all, to dispel a popular misconception, I didn't create Just For Laughs. It was founded by a lawyer-turned-impresario named Gilbert Rozon. Legend has it that in 1982, after a rain-soaked rock festival that he'd promoted turned out to be a disappointing failure,[5] Gilbert's creditors came after him. He gave them a choice: either he'd declare

---

[5] One great memento of that event was a photo of Tina Turner, pouring out her heart and soul in front of about fifteen people at an outdoor concert site that had become a water-logged swamp.

bankruptcy and they'd never see a dime of what they were owed, or they could apply the debt to next year's event. Gilbert was renowned for being a guy with big balls, but this was a lot of chutzpah, even for him. "Are you out of your mind?" the incredulous creditors asked. "Another stiff music festival?" Trying to buy time, Gilbert stammered, "N-n-n-no, it's not a music event. It's a . . . it's a . . ." And then, divine intervention: "It's a comedy festival!"

Given the choice between nothing at all or a slim chance of something, the creditors bought into Gilbert's brainstorm. And, to his extreme credit, Un Festival Juste Pour Rire was launched in July 1983; there were sixteen shows over two nights, all in French except for a concert by an a cappella group called The Nylons. I was writing a column back then for a newspaper called the *Downtowner*, and I actually interviewed Gilbert— entirely in French, as he could barely speak a word of English—in order to mooch Nylons tickets from him. Go figure—a mere eighteen months later we would start a partnership that would last fifteen years and a friendship that endures to this day.

Gilbert and I first met face-to-face in 1985. I had just finished with the Howie Mandel tour, and Gilbert was looking for someone to help get the English-language expansion of his festival off the ground. A master seducer,[6] he convinced me to give up my entertainment-marketing business and come to work on his fledgling, shoestring-budgeted comedy event for the majestic sum of nine thousand dollars. We were a team of six back then, and my responsibilities ran the gamut, from writing press releases to scouting performers to fixing the photocopier to hauling equipment backstage.

Conditions were somewhat less-than-Hollywood in those less-than-halcyon days. Our offices were on top of a grocery store, an Italian restaurant, and the Polish War Veterans Legion Hall. The only elevator in the building was built for freight, not humans, and the nighttime cockroach community was so bountiful that the bugs simply ignored us when we turned on the lights or stamped our feet.

---

[6] How masterful? I once heard him tell a woman, "I'd love to make love to you, but I'm too shy to ask."

Backstage at the St. Denis Theater in 1987. From left to right:
me, Judy Tenuta, Graham Chapman, Gilbert, host David Steinberg,
Richard Belzer, Steven Wright, Rita Rudner,
and a pre Mr. Bean Rowan Atkinson.

But we were happier then, goddammit! Sorry . . . Just a clichéd flashback.

In those days, the idea of a Montreal-based comedy festival made many people laugh, particularly the talent agents in New York and L.A. we were so desperately struggling to impress. We considered ourselves lucky to get through the doors of a few subagents—middlemen who bought talent from big agencies like William Morris and ICM, added their markup, and sold shows to Kiwanis clubs and church fundraisers. (The only reason they agreed to meet with us in the first place was that, in trying to pronounce his name with an English accent, Gilbert would introduce himself as "Rosen"; the Jewish guys we called took pity on a couple of "lanzmen" traipsing about their town.)

The first "real" agent to give the festival the time of day was Bob Williams, who ran a small agency called Spotlite Entertainment in New York. Although many—including yours truly, at the time—questioned his motives, Bob delivered us his A-level talent list, including Jay Leno,

Paul Reiser, Yakov Smirnoff (hey, he was big then!), *Saturday Night Live*'s Kevin Nealon, and a popular young touring comic named Jerry Seinfeld. During the first three years of Just For Laughs, just about every deal we did passed through Bob's hands first. In effect, he was our first representative. He brought us Jerry Lewis in '86 and even schlepped down the block from his West 57th Street offices to the Carnegie Deli where he convinced the late Henny Youngman to appear at the festival in '87. (These days, based in Nashville, Williams runs a thriving worldwide management company that handles, among others, teen faves The Moffats.)

In addition to Williams's clients, Gilbert and I managed to land a number of future heavyweights in the early years. Long before he was Mr. Bean, Rowan Atkinson decimated our audiences with a routine in which he played a hapless subway passenger who is victimized by a wicked invisible man. A brunette Brett Butler, pre-*Grace Under Fire*, viciously skewered her southern roots. But perhaps the mightiest unknown was a skinny teenage kid I would have to beg New York comedy club owners to put on their stages for me to see. At times I would even pay for his transportation to out-of-the-way places like Caroline's at the Seaport in order to make it possible for him to audition for the festival. To his credit, Chris Rock has never forgotten these efforts, and he always goes out of his way to shoot the breeze with me whenever we find ourselves in the same place.

But the best was yet to come.

They say that in humor, timing is everything, and after we'd spent a couple of years learning the ropes in relative obscurity, Just For Laughs was in a prime position to capitalize on the comedy boom that hit showbiz in the late eighties. (One of my favorite maxims of the era, repeated ad nauseum in just about every press report, was, "Comedy is the rock and roll of the eighties.")[7] In 1985 CBC Television signed a contract with us to air a series of festival highlights, and in our years with the Canadian Broadcasting Corporation we learned the TV business. It was Ivan Fecan, now CEO of Bell Globemedia, who gave us our initial break with the network; he also saved our skins by signing us to a long-

---

[7] A few years later the media labeled karaoke "the comedy of the nineties."

term deal in 1990. In 1989, following Just For Laughs' increased media attention in 1988 (see chapter 4), someone from Disney sent a development executive to Montreal to poke around. The exec was impressed by an old buddy of mine, Lenny Clarke, a Boston native. Disney quickly signed him to a "holding deal" (that's showbizese for, "We'll pay you a bunch of money to prevent you from working for anyone else for a period of time, and we hope that someone in our employ can come up with a TV show concept for you before this period ends"). While most of these holding deals send talent on a long journey to oblivion, Lenny's deal miraculously led to an immediate, eponymous CBS sitcom (long before *Roseanne* there was *Lenny*).

That was the proverbial tipping point. Ever see those domino rallies where thousands of little tiles fall in waves? That's what happened, industry-wise, at Just For Laughs. Starting in 1990 and escalating virally each year, every network and studio in Hollywood sent hordes of execs to our talent gold rush. They were looking, if not for the mother lode, then at least to stake their claim.

Although we can't take full credit for their careers (showbiz success is like a plane crash; it's caused by a chain reaction of many smaller incidents), TV and movie stars like Ray Romano, Adam Sandler, Jim Carrey, Kevin James, Drew Carey, Jon Stewart, Norm MacDonald, Denis Leary, Tommy Davidson, Eddie Griffin, Janeane Garofalo, Mark Curry, Eddie Izzard, Rob Schneider, Harland Williams, Lee Evans, and Caroline Rhea all appeared in their nascent professional stages at Just For Laughs.

Perhaps the best, fastest, and longest-running festival success story is Tim Allen. In 1990 Tim was a relatively unknown club comedian. Since I had never seen him deliver a bad joke, let alone have a bad set, and since he had his own upcoming Showtime special to promote, we chose him to be the lead-off act for our Showtime gala that year. Less than fourteen months later Tim was starring on ABC's *Home Improvement*. (I remember meeting Ted Harbert, the ABC entertainment president, in his Century City offices after the L.A. earthquake in 1994. He pointed to his walls lined with slightly tilted photos of Tim, Brett Butler, Steve Harvey, and others. "We've done very well by you," he said. "Great," I replied. "Please share the wealth.")

We didn't just "get 'em while they're young," either. Throughout its history, Just For Laughs presented some of the hottest and most respected names in the history of the comedy genre. George Burns. John Candy. Jonathan Winters. Steve Allen. Milton Berle. Kelsey Grammer. Lily Tomlin. Steven Wright. Nathan Lane. Bob Newhart. Don Rickles. Roseanne. Mary Tyler Moore. David Schwimmer. Barry (Dame Edna Everage) Humphries. Monty Python's Graham Chapman, Eric Idle, and Terry Jones. Richard Belzer. The Smothers Brothers. The type of people I would watch on TV as a kid and dream of one day meeting.

Despite the festival's high proportion of American comedians, the fundamental aim of Just For Laughs was to be an international comedy event. From Edinburgh, Scotland, to Cologne, Germany, to Melbourne, Australia—I would travel to any venue in any country to find something new, and, trust me, I sat in many a dank grungehole in my mostly fruitless attempts to discover a gem.[8] (In fact, after many years, worn out by the process, I came up with an adage to describe international talent hunting: It's like someone tossing a rare black pearl into a whirlpool of excrement; your job is to find it.)

But, no matter what, knowing what it was like to be dumped on, we treated every international contact with the utmost respect. Back in '86 Gilbert warned me not to come across "so American" when dealing with our British clients. Therefore, in a concentrated effort to be more "like them," I would wake up at 4:30 A.M.—taking the five-hour time difference into consideration—and call to do business "on their clock," so to speak. Our conversations always started the same way.

"Are you in town?" was their first question. "No, I'm in Montreal," was my chipper response. This quickly prompted their second question: "Are you nuts?"

For years we only had ourselves to contend with, but the launch of two new comedy events in the early nineties provided Just For Laughs with some enemies to hate. There's nothing better than a war to drive

---

[8] Not everyone appreciated our McLuhan-inspired global-village strategy. I remember the immortal words of Stu Smiley, HBO's VP of comedy programming, following a pitch session for our TV show in 1988: "This international festival is a great idea. Now, if we could only get rid of the foreign shit."

a business—especially a creative one—and we fought bloody battles on both coasts to keep ours on top.

I know it's not nice to call Alan King a prick, but I'm gonna do it anyway. We kissed his ass from sacroiliac to scrotum when he was with us in 1992. We even paid for his New York "assistant" to accompany him throughout his sojourn here. The assistant, actually a top New York promoter, did nothing but take copious notes. A few months after returning home from Just For Laughs on a first-class ticket, King announced the formation of a new comedy event in New York, the Toyota Comedy Festival (brilliant name, Al!), over which he would copreside. To add insult to injury, he didn't even hide the origins of his larceny. "I was up in Montreal last summer," he said. "What's so funny about that city? Since when did it become the comedy center of the universe?" Since you left, pal. Since you left.

A more formidable opponent was the Aspen Comedy Festival. It began as a tiny event run by Brian Murphy, but in 1995 it was pretentiously renamed the U.S. Comedy Arts Festival and pumped up with superstar steroids when HBO became its main patron. Unlike Just For Laughs, which exists first and foremost for the paying public, Aspen is an unabashedly industry-oriented event, a Hollywood schmooze—and, I must admit, it's a damn good one. Local attendance has risen at subsequent incarnations of the Aspen fest, but its primary purpose is still to give showbiz types an opportunity to see-and-be-seen, ski-and-be-seen, and sign-and-be-signed.

For a couple of years Aspen gave us a solid boot to the head, but the insanely competitive nature of Just For Laughs' Bruce Hills[9]—a man so anal-retentive that he doesn't merely ask if the term takes a hyphen, he measures the punctuation mark and checks that it's level—ensured that for every desirable new act Aspen showcased for the gathered industry, we'd feature three.

---

[9] Bruce, who was a student of mine when I taught business courses at Montreal's LaSalle College, joined Just For Laughs in 1986 as a driver. He quickly rose through the ranks to become director of programming while I was around, and his professionalism, attention to detail, and impeccable track record made him the obvious choice to fill my shoes on the English side of the event after I left.

My contribution to the Aspen combat was a little more stealthy and subversive than Bruce's trench warfare. Every year, to mark his Comedy Awards ceremony in Los Angeles, eminent producer George Schlatter (of *Laugh-In* and *Real People* fame) published a souvenir program and gave Just For Laughs a free two-page ad in it. In 1996, as I had done the previous two years, I filled one page with photos and the other with a friendly, somewhat droll, letter. For those who read closely this time around there was a secret message to decipher in my "Nine Reasons to Attend Just For Laughs" note. If they scanned the first letter of each paragraph, bullet pointed for better visibility along the left-hand side of the page, they could decode the carefully hidden acrostic that expressed the sentiment "F.U.C.K.A.S.P.E.N." Juvenile, perhaps, but we all got a good kick out of it back at the ranch.

If you're any good in show business, after a while you become rather adept at tooting your own horn. But, despite all the hype and mass-media massaging, the reality is that not everything we did at Just For Laughs was met with wild cheers, cornucopias of cash, and scatterings of rose petals at our feet; frankly, we fell on our asses as frequently as we soared. But this was all part of the master plan. To maintain our leadership position we had to take risks, and although they stung like hell at the time, our spectacular failures always brought us more than our moderate successes did. Another etched-in-granite festival adage was, "If everything worked, we didn't go far enough." This daredevil attitude was instilled in me from day one by Gilbert, who would frequently call me up just to ask, "Did you make a mistake today?"

As far as mistakes went, perhaps the one that got the most ink in Just For Laughs annals was the International Museum of Humor, which opened its doors on April 1, 1993. And closed them on January 17, 1994. And reopened them in July of the same year. The melodramatic, topsy-turvy story of the museum could be the subject of a book in itself. The project was inspired by a conversation I had in 1989 with a TV executive who disdainfully dissed my beloved festival. That night, incensed and rendered insomniac by the man's lack of respect, I bolted out of bed at 4:00 A.M. and scribbled down ten ideas that would build our esteem. The last read, simply, "Humor Hall of Fame and Museum." I showed the list to Gilbert while we were at the Algonquin Hotel in New York, and

Here's Nine Reasons You Should Attend

This Year

- Fourteen (count 'em!) new acts signed to network or production company deals in 1995 alone. 275 Hollywood jobs saved or justified in the process.
- Unfathomingly weak Canadian dollar makes hemming the pants the most expensive part of the Armani suits you'll bring back.
- Cuban cigars and Chez Paree: still legal. Speaking English: uh, well...
- Kinder, gentler Bruce Hills.
- Andy Nulman promises not to wear his striped pants; Rick Messina unveils his new baseball cap; Jim Kellem will probably go topless.
- Still the only place where VIP passes are free (well, to most), where beer is as strong as tequila and where Jamie Masada's accent doesn't stand out that much.
- Perhaps the last year to visit Canada while it's still Canada. And threat of separation still less dangerous than threat of earthquakes, fires, floods or riots.
- Extra ice cube added to Club Soda air conditioning system.
- Next year, you too will be able to understand these inside jokes!

Just For Laughs
The Montreal International
Comedy Festival
14th Year
...and still the largest comedy event
in the world!
July 17-28, 1996

(514) 845-3155 for information, reservations
or if you just need to talk to a sympathetic soul
like Willie Mercer or Robin Altman

43

Stealth revenge: my secret message acrostic ad in the
1996 American Comedy Awards program.

he instantly jumped on idea number ten. For the next three years the museum would become Gilbert's obsession, consuming almost all of his time and energy.

Like most projects of such grandeur, the museum went overbudget and ran late, yet it suffered most from its own raison d'être—ironic as it sounds, nobody would take the idea of a comedy museum seriously. Add to this a comment Gilbert made at the groundbreaking ceremony: "This will be the first museum not dependent on government money." You could almost hear the collective "ka-shinng!" of the long knives being unsheathed by the assembled media (who would thrust them with extreme meticulousness when the museum faltered and we had to seek public funds).

In retrospect the museum, once opened, was actually quite hip. Installed in a converted heritage brewery, it housed a walk-through history of humor, where audio and video clips were played within soaring, three-dimensional, Disney-style sets. But the die had already been cast—the perception of the project had already solidified as one of excess, waste, and frivolity. To me the shocker wasn't that it closed, it's that we ever managed to open it in the first place. Today the museum complex houses the Just For Laughs offices, and the museum still presents the odd exhibit, usually kid-oriented. But it doesn't approach the castle in the sky that Gilbert spent over three years of his life dreaming up, developing, and trying to deliver.

So, as you can see—and as James Taylor sang—"I've seen fire and I've seen rain." For fifteen years I busted my balls so that others could have fun. The rewards were great (without Just For Laughs, what would you be reading now? Another Stephen King book?), but the path we had to take to claim them was far north of Easy Street. Everything we did had to satisfy not one, but eight target markets,[10] which is why I called the event's organizing process "spinning the octopus"; one false move and you're strangled by a tentacle. Every July we put on an Olympic Games–sized logistical nightmare of a happening, and then we'd

---

[10] I'll never forget them: the ticket-buying public, the media, our sponsors, the TV networks and their viewers, the government, the performers themselves, the industry, and, of course, ourselves.

start from scratch to build the next one, even before the current one had actually gotten under way. Yet up until my last days as Just For Laughs CEO, people were still coming up to me to ask, "Yeah, but what do you do the rest of the year?" The fact that I'm free to write this book in the confines of my second-floor study instead of a subterranean jail cell is a testament to my patience and the rock-solid scar tissue on my lower lip.

Bitter? Nah—how could I be? By the time I had my last laugh at the festival, my baby had grown to span almost a full month, with hundreds of shows, thousands of performers, attendance figures of over 1.5 million, and a worldwide TV audience of tens of millions more. Leaving on a high, I bid adieu to my friends and second family in September 1999. It was my moment to turn the page and move on to something new. And now it's yours.

T H R E E

A FEW OF
MY FAVORITE THINGS

One of the problems with working in comedy is that you gradually become jaded with laughter and those who generate it. After I'd spent so many years at Just For Laughs, my life became the embodiment of the old joke about the gynecologist who, after a hard day at work, is greeted at home by his wife, radiant in sheer silk lingerie. "Aw, please honey," he groans. "If I see one more . . ."

This twisted parable explains the degeneration of my sense of humor from "funny ha-ha" to "funny huh?" Whereas I fully respected the big stars we booked to perform at Just For Laughs for their numerous accomplishments, their reputations, and their larger-than-life auras, they were never my favorite festival performers. While I could appreciate the unadulterated brilliance of a Chris Rock, a Bill Hicks, or a Richard Jeni, being exposed to droves of their less-talented stand-up brethren eventually left me calloused and desensitized to the craft. True confession time: like the sexual deviant who can only perform with amputee redhead midgets, I was only really moved by the freaks and crazies.

So, you can keep your Oscar and Emmy winners. Go ahead and suck up to the sexy sitcom star. Just leave me here with my trove of oddballs, weirdos, and freakniks. Although my mere words may not do them total justice, here are some of my faves.

What goes down must come up: Stevie Starr prepares to swallow
something strange prior to regurgitation.

STEVIE STARR

Equally repulsive and fascinating, Stevie's sobriquet was The Regurgitator. This was truth in advertising, pure and simple—Stevie swallowed stuff and brought it back up again. But he was no mere public bulimic; instead of food, Stevie regurgitated objects like pocket change, lightbulbs, live goldfish, and Rubik's cubes (somehow changing the color configurations on the way up).[11] Yes, folks, *that's* entertainment!

I first saw Stevie in the spring of 1988, in England, in the green room of the *Jonathan Ross Show*. Stevie was scheduled to appear on this popular "chat show" (that's Brit for "talk show"), and his manager, Mike Malley—a sweet guy, but blessed with all the subtlety of a grizzled carney barker—set up a preshow meeting. Gawky, with a crop of carrot-colored hair, Stevie was excruciatingly shy upon being introduced to me. But once Mike put a lightbulb between Stevie's lips, his humility disappeared. Before my astonished eyes, Stevie sucked back the bulb as if it was a Cherrystone oyster. Then he asked me if I had any change. I offered him a handful of coins, among them three fifty-pence pieces. Each had a different date, which he asked me to take note of. Once by one, the coins dove down his gullet, clinking against the lightbulb in his stomach. Then, matter-of-factly, Stevie asked, "Which one do you want brought up first?"

By the time he was through, he had regurgitated all of the coins, one by one, in the order I'd specified, each time opening his mouth wide to show me that nothing was hidden. Then, to top it off, Stevie brought up the lightbulb, puffing his cheeks before disgorging it into his outstretched hands with a flourish. Bravo! What's for dessert? A toaster? Obviously, this was a man after my own heart. Even more obviously, I booked him on the spot.

Violin time. Despite its grotesque nature, Stevie's act has heartbreakingly poignant origins. Stevie grew up in a tough Glasgow orphanage— not an ideal home for anyone, let alone a frail, geeky redhead. Every week the orphans were given a few coins each to spend on candy; naturally, Stevie was the target of the bigger boys, who smacked him

---

[11] Some naysayer, upon seeing Stevie perform this feat at Just For Laughs, scoffed and said, "He doesn't really change the configuration. He just has another Rubik's cube down there and brings up that one instead."

around and stole his money. The only safe place to hide his loot was within, and bringing it up through his esophagus was a whole lot easier than expelling it via the alternative method. He moved on to swallowing other objects and began using this talent to win over his tormentors. Great story. I only hope it's not a figment of Mike Malley's Colonel Parker-esque imagination.

Anyway, on with the show! In an unabashed attempt to amortize the cost of flying Stevie overseas in 1988, I booked him not only for a standard gala set but also to be the opening act for The Reduced Shakespeare Company's theatrical run. This made great financial sense, but artistically it was a match made in hell. Coming to my senses (once the show was sold out, of course), I realized that the RSC's target market, tweed-wearing intellectuals and college students, would be repulsed by this mutant—which is why I cowardly avoided the show's premiere. But, being the masochist that I am, I went to the theater to gauge the mood of the exiting crowd. I approached one wealthy-looking middle-aged woman and asked her how she'd liked the show. "Oh, the Shakespeare boys were all right," she said nonchalantly, before breaking into a happy glow—"But I just loved the magician who opened!"

Be he abnormality or be he sorcerer, Stevie Starr became a festival darling, and he proved himself as adept at swallowing attention as he was at swallowing household objects. He'd perform in elevators, at the bar—wherever he was stopped by the curious. He also inspired two great festival jokes. The first centered on another Stevie (Steven, actually) Starr attending the festival, a William Morris agent. One of his clients, TV producer Jim Valleley, said that the difference between the two was that this Starr would swallow a dollar but bring up ninety cents.[12] The second joke focused on Stevie's religion. With the name Starr, people debated whether or not he was Jewish. "Couldn't be," was the consensus. The reasoning? "He swallows."

UNO LANKA

As a hockey goalie and a passionate snowboarder, I can boast of having a fairly acute sense of balance. Compared to Uno Lanka, however, I'm

---

[12] For those of you who aren't showbiz savvy, agents skim ten percent off their clients' revenues. Get it now?

the proverbial one-legged man in a blindfolded ass-kicking contest. A cross between a gyroscope and a magnet, Uno makes everything he touches onstage seem to defy gravity and physics. But even more impressive than his uncanny equilibrium is the way that he took this marginal, obscure talent, added a dash of raw musicianship, and created an act that has wowed 'em the world over.

During my *Sunday Express* days, I caught Uno in one of those music-hall-type shows that tour the ritzy-but-tacky hotel circuit (hey, a free supper is a free supper). A standout among the bad singers and the half-dressed women too old for the Folies-Bergère, Uno played a flute on which he balanced a golf club vertically, on top of which he balanced another golf club horizontally. To a young, inebriated journalist, that's goddam impressive.

Uno popped back into my life fifteen years later, when his manager, Dave Belenzon (a kind soul with the strange, irritating habit of overpronouncing the three syllables of his last name—"Belll-ennn-zonnn"), casually mentioned him along with about a dozen other acts he was trying to sell me for the 1991 event. My overly enthusiastic reaction and immediate booking must've shocked Belenzon; I mean, I'm sure the response was somewhat less zealous to this powder-blue-jumpsuited balancing act over at *The Tonight Show* and *Letterman*.

On July 19, like a father watching his kid perform in a high school variety show, I "schepped naches" (a Yiddish term literally meaning "I carried pride") as Uno took to the gala stage. And my protégé did not disappoint. His eye-popping finale consisted of the following steps:

1. Balance a soccer-size blue rubber ball on a standard violin bow protruding horizontally from the mouth.
2. Balance an inverted wine goblet on the ball.
3. Place a three-inch-by-eight-inch plate of glass on top of the inverted goblet.
4. Place two more inverted goblets on top of the plate glass.
5. Repeat step 3.
6. Repeat step 4.
7. Repeat step 3.
8. Repeat step 4.
9. Top the whole thing off with a wine goblet with a red rose in it.

Uno Lanka: a sense of balance that defies gravity and
other laws of physics.

Impressive, no? The crowd went wild. And then the unthinkable happened. The tower started to tip. The crowd gasped. But Uno moved
with, not against, the glass spire until it was once again steadfast and
unwavering. A man who'd just missed being an accident victim or a
Barnum-esque showman? Only my Sri Lankan friend knows for sure.

But wait—there's more! As the cherry on the sundae, Uno was
handed a violin, and he rubbed it upside down against the bow (bet
you forgot about that baton, didn't you?) until it produced some notes.
But not just any notes: he played the first two bars of the Jewish folk
ditty "Hava Nagila" before being joined by the full festival band for the
grandest of grand finales. Naches? To schepp any more I would've
needed a forklift.

YOGI DANIEL
Another standout from the Belll-ennn-zonnn brigade was Yogi Daniel,
a contortionist—but not your average, run-of-the-mill, Cirque du Soleil
underaged female Chinese waif contortionist. Yogi was a strapping, clas-
sically handsome Iranian who could do to his body what an Atlantic City

candy maker does to saltwater taffy. To put it another way, remember that sixties blacklight cartoon poster of a man with his head stuck up his rectum? Well, Yogi could've been the model.

Yogi was an equal-opportunity crowd pleaser when he appeared in 1993; his ball-busting warm-up stretches had the males in the audience moaning in sympathy pain, while his animal impressions, most notably the "backwards crab," filled female minds with fantasies and questions. And, like all great showmen, Yogi knew how to kill 'em with the closing number.

Not a man of many words, Yogi would chirp, "This is my house!" as a small lucite box, no bigger than your standard fourteen-inch TV set, was wheeled onstage. Its front side was hinged halfway, and as Yogi flipped it open you realized what he was attempting to do—you just couldn't believe he'd actually be able to do it. I'll spare you the muscle-popping, spine-snapping, testicle-tweaking details. Suffice it to say, the act culminated with a stagehand closing the door as Yogi pulled his

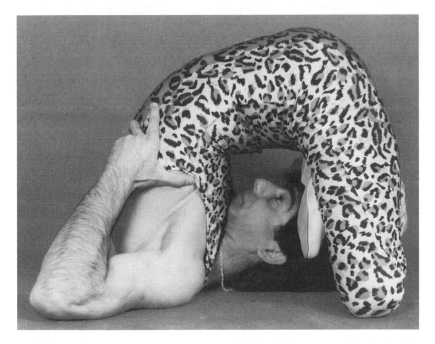

Yogi Daniel: the Iranian contortionist filled minds with "How does he do that?" questions . . . and "I wish I could do that!" fantasies.

double-jointed foot inside the steamy crystal cube. After the box was spun to prove that his entire body was really inside, the door popped open and Yogi spilled out like a baby from the birth canal. Funny ha-ha? No. But funny holy jumpin' Jesus? You bet.

An interesting coda: We had originally booked Yogi for the 1991 festival, but he was a no-show. The reason? Irony of ironies, because of visa problems, he couldn't get into the country. If I knew then what I know now, I would've just shipped the guy via FedEx.

THE GREATEST SHOW ON LEGS

Three years after Malcolm Hardee caused quite the stir by walking onto a Club Soda stage completely naked to light Chris Lynam's anal rocket (see chapter 7), he was back to cause an even bigger stir on an even bigger stage. This time the bespectacled, stalactite-testicled, oft-intoxicated British anarchist would perform a little dance number. But scandal can wait. First, a little history.

Malcolm was the notorious owner of Up the Creek, a dank, smoky, London-area underground comedy club. To subdue loutish, drunken hecklers, he would waddle onstage unclothed, pendulous balls hanging grotesquely about his knees, and urinate on them. If that didn't work (talk about tough crowds!), he'd resort to throwing ashtrays or beer glasses.[13] Despite, or perhaps because of, this conduct, Malcolm was a cult hero on England's alternative comedy scene.

We hadn't officially invited Malcolm over in 1990; he paid his own way and was relatively well behaved. These two factors were critical to us in taking the plunge and inviting him back. There were times when I nearly regretted the decision, especially during a reception at the British consul general's residence in Montreal, held to honor the diplomat's comedic countrymen participating in the festival. Malcolm, decked out in stained, tattered black jacket and jeans, sat alone in blissful, timid detachment throughout. Upon leaving he finally broke his silence by whispering, "Thanks for the silverware" to his host.

---

[13] Needless to say, this was not the favorite place of British performers to showcase for Just For Laughs. And it's just as well, because I was way too intimidated even to set foot in this asylum.

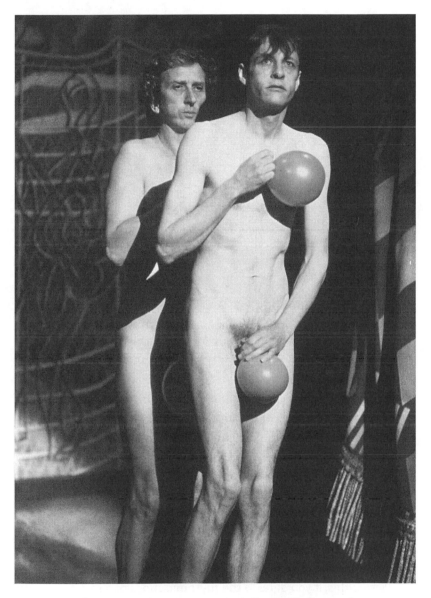

The Greatest Show on Legs: a tentative Martin Soan and
Steve Bowditch cover up modestly.

What do you do for an encore? Soan and Bowditch,
joined by Malcolm Hardee, decide to let it all hang out.

But in '93, Malcolm wasn't serving as Lynam's sideman. He'd come
to the festival as leader of a dance trio called The Greatest Show on
Legs, also featuring Martin Soan and Steve Bowditch. And the popular
reaction to his ballsy ballet, entitled The Balloon Dance, would render
Twyla Tharp or George Balanchine emerald with envy. Now let's put
things in perspective. In a seedy London club, The Balloon Dance might
have been construed as mischievous, maybe even kind of cute. But to
a well-heeled gala audience in the St. Denis Theater, in front of TV
cameras, sponsors, and government officials, the act was potentially
disgraceful. Okay, so much for the disclaimer. Let the good times roll!

Picture this, if you dare. To the rhythmic chops of a samba-cha-cha
instrumental, two pale, emaciated Brits—Soan and Bowditch—appear
onstage clad only in black socks, clutching two inflated kiddie balloons
to cover their privates and nipples. After shuffling side-to-side for a
few notes, the guys whistle for Hardee. Also naked, pale, socked, and
ballooned (but more bloated and scarred), Malcolm joins the conga

line. Every few bars, the guys—in unison—rapidly switch their crotch and chest balloons. Then one of Malcolm's balloons pops. To compensate, he snatches a balloon from one of his partners, causing a clutch-and-grab chain reaction. Amazingly, through it all they maintain their composure and the choreography. The act goes on like this until the guys exit the stage, balloonless, but modestly hiding their scrotal areas with their hands.

The audience response was unlike any I've ever experienced. They loved it. They gasped in bewilderment upon seeing the first two guys, but Hardee's brilliantly timed entrance truly raised the roof. Each balloon switch was greeted with ear-piercing shrieks, sounding more like what you'd hear from a bunch of panic-stricken roller-coaster riders than a comedy-show crowd. People were literally falling out of their seats. It was almost a religious experience.

What do you do for an encore? Well, when hauled back onstage for a curtain call by host Michael Richards, the trio—hands still strategically placed—bowed to the conquered masses and ran back off. But the cheers wouldn't stop, so the guys made one more appearance, running onstage and jumping to show their appreciation. And, put it this way, this time they waved to the crowd. With both hands. I've lived through earthquakes, so I know what it feels like: the ground actually shook.

Richards, who for years played Seinfeld's flustered sidekick, pulled a real-life Kramer that night. Speechless, he giggled until he could spit out these words: "I think I saw his pee-pee!" Perhaps the best reactions to this encore of encores were the ones captured by our TV director, Ron Meraska. We didn't witness them until weeks later, when the tape of the show was being edited.[14] Ronnie had caught people shielding their eyes, people convulsing with laughter, and people pointing. But his very best shot focused on a woman in the first balcony who calmly reached into her purse . . . and pulled out a pair of binoculars.

---

[14] It's no surprise that this bit made great TV. It was so good that gritty ol' Malcolm was nominated in 1994 for a Best Performance in a Music, Comedy, or Variety Special or Series Gemini Award.

JANGO EDWARDS

In the decade and a half that I spent at Just For Laughs, I played host to thousands of artists of all types from all over the world. Most came and went without even registering a ripple. Some caused a commotion or a calamity. But no single performer provoked the kind of mass frenzy that Jango Edwards did.

Describing Jango is like describing an ephemeral emotion. Though he appears in the flesh (like Hardee, many times literally), he is an intangible entity. For festival press releases we culled quotes from French and Dutch sources, calling him things like, "a madman's wet dream," "forbidden fruit that bites back," "rock and roll, guerilla theater, and Marat Sade," and, "a cross between The Ringling Brothers and *A Clockwork Orange*." Want more? The *New York Times* said that Jango "makes John Belushi look like Charlie Brown." The *Hollywood Reporter* insisted he's "not a native of this planet." Even the pretentious *Village Voice* waxed poetic: "Skelton, Marceau, and the Brothers Ritz and Marx have informed him, but they register naïve beside his conscious dance with ambivalence." Translator, please.

Jango was the creation of Stanley Ted Edwards, a landscape artist from Detroit. Inspired by a book on self-awareness and/or forty hits of acid, he left his hometown in 1969, took up residence in free-love-era Europe, and became the quintessential kamikaze klown. Tall, hook-nosed, with a flowing ebony mane, Jango was an exhibitionist Howard Stern with rhythm. His concert act,[15] which had its North American premiere with us in 1988, consisted of hallucinatory, sexually depraved sketches and songs backed by the wildly costumed Big Nose Band. A one-man circus of the absurd, Jango morphed into clown monsters like Ali Baba, The Great Retardo, and Mr. Noisse, all savage lampoons of standard comedic characters. The show's finale featured a fast-talkin' Jango in a grotesque Fat Elvis costume launching into a version of "Come Go with Me" before jumping out of the sponge-cellulite ensemble. Then, as the band played a daredevil's crescendo, Jango, wearing only a

---

[15] A Dutch newspaper compared it to "a wild evening at the fair, where all the rides are set in the highest gear, and when someone appears to get nauseous, the pace is upped even more."

winged, sequined G-string, mounted a chair and dove headfirst into a Dixie cup filled with water.

How can you possibly top that? Well, for his encore Jango came onstage alone as a nude male geisha, his genitals tucked between his legs, and shuffled across the stage, oh-so-deliberately. And, when the lights went up, he raced to the front of the hall, clad only in a worn bathrobe, to meet and greet the people he'd just enthralled, provoked, and/or revolted. Wild!

Yet Jango's offstage antics were even wilder. He would crawl around on all fours like a dog, sniffing and licking people as they cautiously passed by. He would wander along the edges of sidewalk cafes and gauge the temperature of the patrons' coffees with his finger. In restaurants he would pretend to kill imaginary flies and eat them slowly, crunching with each bite. He would bark out his hotel room number to every female within hearing distance and announce it during every radio and TV interview he did; as a result, his Delta Hotel quarters were busier than the lobby bar, twenty-four hours a day. The Energizer Bunny stared at him with envy.

Despite being ravaged by the critics, Jango's Live show was such a hit that government officials joined members of the general public in begging us for tickets. One night producer Bob Kaminsky and I shoehorned a couple of HBO executives into the back of the room. Before the show was half over, they insisted that we find a way to get Jango onto our live TV broadcast hosted by John Candy. Obviously, nobody could follow this whirlwind, so Jango closed the TV show, and he did so with the Elvis/dive number (ironically, he was forced to wear a flap on the back of his G-string, lest his bare ass offend the sensitive viewers of America's premier uncensored pay service). Even though Jango infected a handful of us with colds through his incessant licking, everyone at Just For Laughs loved him in 1988.

That's why we decided to do it all over again in 1989. But with a twist. A theater alone wasn't big enough to contain Jango Edwards. So, borrowing a concept I'd seen Australian comedian Rod Quantock enact (quite boringly, I might add) in Melbourne a year before, I unleashed Jango on the entire city with an adventure called Looney Tours (or, as we labeled it, "A cross between Ken Kesey's School Bus, the Beatles'

Jango Edwards: a one-man circus of the absurd.

Magical Mystery Tour, and *Les Misérables*"). It was simple—in principle, at least. Jango (along with buddies-in-anarchy Justin Case, Johnny Melville, and Rick Parets) would lead one hundred people on a ninety-minute bus-and-walking tour of Montreal, pointing out memorable sites and relating interesting tidbits along the way. But nothing was ever simple with Jango. His cast bloated to twenty members, his costume and prop budgets expanded exponentially (on each bus ride they used up a case of Silly String, which festival assistant Willie Mercer had to scrape laboriously from windows and seats each morning), and his disrespect for the city's sites increased in direct proportion to their historical relevance.

I took part in the "dress rehearsal," and the experience left me aghast. The tour started with a very wet frat-house version of *Hamlet* ("Two beers? Or not two beers?"), continued with a talk show hosted by Jango as Jesus Christ on a foam-rubber crucifix (this just below Montreal's famed Mount Royal cross landmark), and followed up with a flare-gun battle in the square just outside the ancient Notre Dame Cathedral. The whole mess culminated in the majestic fountain next to City Hall, where the cast cavorted in bathing suits while Jango splashed through the water totally naked—save for the swinging seven-foot rubber penis attached to his natural member.

By this time I knew that the tour wasn't going to make any money, but after rolling home in a bus covered in sticky pink goo, three of its windows already broken, I felt the pressure of impending crucifixion myself. We were doomed.

The last stop on the tour was the Delta Hotel, and I planned to be anywhere but there on opening night. But it turned out that Jerry Seinfeld was checking in that evening, and I had to be on hand. As fate would have it, the battered bus pulled up at the side entrance just after I'd sent the future billionaire up to his suite. A group of weary, shell-shocked tour participants stumbled from the bus and went their separate ways. "Oh, no," I thought. "I'm going to be sued again." Just then a local newsman named Robert Vairo emerged from the vehicle. Vairo was a crusty type, numbed from too many years working in media, and, sure enough, he caught my eye and made a beeline to where I stood shuddering.

"How was it?" I asked weakly, not really wanting to hear his response. "It was incredible!" blurted Vairo. I waited for the sarcastic follow-up, but instead he enthused, "You have a real hit on your hands. I can't wait to do a piece on this."

Yes, I guess there is a comedy God. Sometimes it just takes the comedy devil to bring him out of hiding. Good work, Jango.[16]

KLAUS MYERS

The year 1990 was indeed an exciting one. It marked the end of one of the world's coldest cold war symbols, the Berlin Wall. After the dust settled, three distinct entities emerged that stood to benefit most from the fact that the odious structure had come crashing to the ground: East Germans, capitalism . . . and Jim Myers.

If Jim were a ballplayer, he'd be the popular, light-hitting journeyman who alternates between the majors and the minors for a few years before drifting out of professional sport altogether. But he was a comedian, and as a comedian he gigged on the club circuit as a competent middle act; he never had the chops to achieve Seinfeldian success in either stand-up or sitcoms.

What Jim did have, however, was chiseled Aryan features and a killer opening number that took advantage of them. He'd be introduced as "Klaus Myers," and, with perfect Germanic pacing and accent, he'd perform a brief, somewhat clichéd fish-out-of-water routine. (Opening line: "I am pleased to meet you. My name is Klaus Myers. I am from Germany. And my motto is, 'Let bygones be bygones.'") After about seven minutes he'd segue out of the character into his real voice, surprise his audience, and move on to his more pedestrian mainstream act. So, let's put two and two together: I run an international festival. The Berlin Wall has fallen. What better way to exploit the situation than with a German comic? Hello Klaus, and goodbye Jim.

Actually, that was the rule: Jim was to be known exclusively as Klaus throughout his time at the event. He was billed exclusively as Klaus, we added Germany to the official list of participating countries, and when he wasn't performing, he was to lie as low as possible. A

---

[16] Incidentally, Jango made one final appearance at Just For Laughs in 1994 as part of the ill-fated Gala 5. But that, dear readers, is a whole other story in a whole other chapter.

Jim (Klaus) Myers benefited big time from the fall of the Berlin Wall.

realist, Jim took it all in stride. He understood that without Klaus, he'd probably never get to be more than a spectator at this festival. What's more, as Klaus, he got to appear alongside Tim Allen and Weird Al Yankovic on our live Showtime broadcast, hosted by Bob Newhart. They say that comedy's all about timing, and Jim was unquestionably in the right place at the right time.

Saturday, July 21. Gala time. Veteran *Saturday Night Live* designer Leo Yoshimura had assembled an astonishing set for our "German" guest—an open barricade in front of a replica of the Brandenburg Gate. Jim had never performed in a theater this size and in front of a crowd this big, never mind in front of five thousand dollars' worth of art and props created just for him. But, like the journeyman ballplayer who hits that one game-winning homer, Jim/Klaus replicated the destruction of the Wall and reduced the crowd to a pile of rubble. He had them from his first joke. "I would like to settle your minds concerning this ridiculous notion that Germans are obsessed with mathematical uniformity. This is a total fabrication. Now . . . ahem . . ." He paused for a split second before delivering his knockout. "Joke number one: Take my wife—I command you!"

The moment was truly magic. Not only did the audience laugh uproariously, but they were also emotionally moved, and they embraced this stiff, blond comedic ambassador with warmth, respect, and a standing ovation. Not bad for a New Jersey guy accustomed to playing to tourists, drunks, and drunken tourists.

Hindsight is twenty-twenty, but right up until the moment Jim was to step onstage as Klaus, a major controversy was going on behind the scenes over whether he should reveal that his act was just an act. Charlie Joffe, Woody Allen's manager and film producer, was working with us as a creative consultant for the Showtime TV show, and he was adamant that either Newhart or Jim himself should spill the beans after the performance. I was even more adamant that they shouldn't.

"What, we're gonna be arrested by the reality police?" I protested. "Screw reality! It's like wrestling, and he's playing a character." Joffe, putting all his years of experience into his phrasing, warned ominously, "People are going to be really pissed off. They don't like to be fooled." Well, Charlie, until now, they never knew they were.

TOKYO SHOCK BOYS

I've said many times that underneath every comedian is a manic depressive, but at least you know which obsession is the driving force behind his or her art. As for performers of the ilk described in this chapter—new vaudevillians, novelty acts, call them what you will—it takes more than a shrink to identify the demons that motivate their creative zeal. This is a job for an exorcist! But even the Jesuit priest who did wonders for little Linda Blair in *The Exorcist* would be no match for The Tokyo Shock Boys. Swallowing coins or climbing into small boxes I can understand, but when it comes to these guys, I still find myself wondering, "Why?"

Like The Regurgitator, The Tokyo Shock Boys lived up to their name, verbatim. They were four distinct characters: an evil-looking sadist (the group's leader); a tall dimwit; a bald daredevil; and, finally, for lack of a better term, a human sacrifice. Their act, if you could call it that, was a bizarre mélange of music and masochism, performed with a smile. Decked out in loud Japanese garb, the Boys would make their entrance dancing to a staccato/drone version of The Surfaris' classic "Wipe Out." And then things would get weird. Imagine, if your mind can descend to

The Tokyo Shock Boys: quiet, refined cultural ambassadors of the Orient.

the bowels of depravity, the trials and tribulations that went into developing this set list:

- Daredevil enters wearing a toupee. Dimwit sets it on fire.
- Dimwit punches self in stomach. Sacrifice holds a lighter to Dimwit's rectum, which explodes in flame as he passes gas.
- Sacrifice wears a diaper filled with fireworks.[17] Dimwit lights it. Sacrifice dances as it explodes.
- Dimwit eats a handful of dry ice.
- Daredevil holds screaming firecracker in his hand. It explodes.
- Daredevil holds screaming firecracker in his teeth. It explodes.
- Daredevil jams screaming firecrackers up his nostrils. They explode.
- Sacrifice wraps rubber tubing around his scrotum and pulls a platform loaded with audience members.
- Sacrifice climbs into an oversized plastic bag. Sadist sucks the air out with a vacuum, leaving Sacrifice looking like a freeze-dried raisin.
- And then the showstopper: the music climbs to a deafening crescendo as Sadist barks out orders; Dimwit Crazy Glues a hammer to his face and dives into the audience; Daredevil Crazy Glues his bald head to the naked butt of a dancing Sacrifice, and the two leave the stage dancing as one.

Ahhh . . . I just can't get enough of that refined oriental culture!

Needless to say, when I received an unsolicited demo tape of the Boys' fun and games, I rushed to show it to everyone in the office. Their combined reaction of intrigue and revulsion made it clear to me that the Boys were a sure bet; they'd be the most successful showbiz quartet since The Beatles.

So sue me—I was off by a bit. Maybe The Tokyo Shock Boys, like their Panasonic brethren, were "just slightly ahead of our time." Tom

---

[17] One problem we faced was that customs officers wouldn't let the Boys bring their fireworks into the country, so we had to buy them domestic replacements. But, like our beer, the local stuff was a little stronger than what the guys were used to. Whoops! Sorry . . .

Green is now making a career out of this brand of sadomasochist humor, but in 1992 audiences were still shocked by Andrew Dice Clay (the Eminem of his time, kids). Not everyone, shall we say, appreciated what the Boys did onstage, but those who liked it—a degenerate group that included yours truly, legendary British producer Geoff Posner, and pre-TV-star Drew Carey[18]—liked it a lot.

Offstage, The Tokyo Shock Boys were a classic study in human contradiction. Despite Sacrifice's strange habit of walking around with a bottle of mineral water stuck to his forehead (bowing politely to pour drinks for whomever would partake), the Boys were shy and respectful, almost demure. They made no demands and enjoyed all the attention. Low maintenance all the way. What's more, following Japanese tradition, they came bearing gifts; I managed to score a silk kimono, a digital Sony Walkman, and a set of cufflinks embossed with couples in different fornicatory positions (when I opened the box, the Boys snickered and covered their mouths like schoolgirls at a convent).

Perhaps the most extraordinary moment of their stay came during an interview I had to do for Japanese television. The Shock Boys' arrival on Western shores was such a big deal back home in the Land of the Rising Sun that a TV documentary crew was on hand to capture their every move (their manager, Janet Hasegawa, even requested that I lead a sign-carrying welcome party of about a hundred people to greet the Boys at the airport). With the Boys peering over at me from a hotel-room couch located behind the cameraman, I was asked what had inspired me to bring them overseas. "That's easy," I replied. "After seeing so many boring acts, I get turned on by something this insane."

There was a pause as a Japanese translator converted my words. Then all of a sudden the Boys recoiled in horror. The director jumped up and yelled, "Cut!"—or something to that effect. The situation degenerated into a pandemonium of screeching and hand signals. Had I been disrespectful to other acts by calling them "boring"? Had I been too sexually forward by using the term "turned on"? Not even close. When

---

[18] Drew was so taken by the Boys that he even volunteered to sub for Sacrifice in the vacuum bag at Club Soda during a Late Night Danger Zone show. To this day, every time I catch Drew on TV, I can't help but think how horrified his current-day handlers and insurers would be to see him shriveled and nearly asphyxiated.

the dust settled, I learned what had lit the fuse for this most thunder-
ous of explosions. On Japanese TV, while it's perfectly okay to use your
testes as a towing device or show a guy gluing his head to another
guy's naked ass, using the word "insane" is forbidden.

F O U R

HOW SWEET IT IS: JOHN CANDY

The year 1988 marked the turning point for Just For Laughs. Our pleasant, thriving local event had vaulted to the status of international comedic powerhouse. Jango Edwards and Stevie "The Regurgitator" Starr made their debut festival appearances that year; we also introduced non-stand-up shows, and, most notably, we made the decision to close off a block of downtown streets and feature free outdoor performances. These street performances were the epitome of win-win: they helped to increase the festival's attendance figures dramatically, and the teeming masses that gathered to watch made us more attractive to sponsors.

But sponsors don't just want numbers. They want heat. And, compared to years past, 1988 proved to be an inferno. Ironically, two expatriate Canadians were most responsible for flooding our spark with gasoline: Montreal native Marty Klein, then the president of the mighty Agency for the Performing Arts (we'll call it APA) and one of his A-list clients, Toronto's John Candy.

Only a year earlier, the biggest star Just For Laughs could muster was David Steinberg. (Another Canadian! Jeez, these guys are everywhere.) While Steinberg is bright and personable, his performance as 1987 gala host was met with yawns and snores. One local critic damned the poor guy with the faintest of praise, saying, "Steinberg and his wit are admired by dozens and dozens of people around the world." With Steinberg at the helm, the best we could do TV-wise was get some lunch money from Showtime (about $175,000) for a show nobody much cared about. To compound a sad situation, Steinberg insisted on being lit by a distant, balcony-mounted white spotlight (no colored stage wash at all), and convinced many others on the show to follow suit. The end result was a dreary, almost melancholy, comedy special,[19] one we knew we would have a hard time even giving away the following year.

I had never produced a TV show entirely by myself, but when Gilbert offered up the opportunity I knew I could do better than our 1987 offering. Over the winter I met with a number of producers, and I became enamored with Bob Kaminsky, who had worked for Bette Midler and David Bowie, among others. Kaminsky introduced me to Paul Miller, one of the world's top live-TV directors, who was then directing *Saturday Night Live*. What a farce—I had a topflight producer and director but no show.

Enter Marty.

We had booked a couple of smaller APA clients in '86 and '87, which put us on Marty Klein's radar screen. A comedy lover who had discovered Steve Martin and was the first agent brave enough to sign Sam Kinison, Marty was intrigued by this event bubbling in his hometown. He asked Glenn Schwartz (who did PR duties for many members of the APA stable) about it, and Glenn responded by setting the two of us up for a meeting in New York in the early spring of '88, that exceptional year.

I met with Marty and his partner, Roger Vorce, at a bustling bistro. The two shook their heads in sympathy as I went on about the festival's illustrious past and its less-than-whopping TV deals. "How would you like it," Marty offered, "if you were on HBO, with John Candy hosting your show?" I didn't reply immediately. I waited for Marty to sprout horns and ask for my soul in return. "What's the catch?" I finally asked, trying my best to sound showbiz savvy.

---

[19] However, the '87 show did mark the North American television debut of Craig Ferguson, who plays Drew Carey's boss on Carey's ABC sitcom. Ferguson performed an aggressive rant under the unfortunate stage name of "Bing Hitler."

"No catch," came Marty's reply. "I like what you're doing, and [then HBO president] Michael Fuchs is a friend. I think I can deliver John, and we've got a show." We? We've got a show? I couldn't believe it. One of the most powerful men in show business wanted to represent Just For Laughs and bring one of Hollywood's hottest stars along for the ride. From that moment until his untimely death in 1992, Marty Klein became the festival's best friend and my mentor.

Two days later Marty delivered on his end of the bargain. Not just a one-year deal, but a two-year deal with HBO, cable TV's most prestigious network, for a colossal $600,000. That's $600,000 *per year!* What's more, the show would be broadcast live across the USA in July as the festival's culminating event. Now, however, there was a catch: no John Candy, no show. Since he last appeared on the network, as host of its eighth annual *Young Comedians' Special*, Candy had become a megastar. More importantly for HBO, he was also a movie star (TV welcomes film stars a lot more warmly than film welcomes TV stars). But if Marty could deliver a $1.2 million contract in two days, getting his client onboard was a done deal, right? Wrong.

"I can recommend he do it," Marty told me, "but you've got to do the work. I set up a meeting at his house two weeks from now. It's up to you to convince him." So, basically, the whole house of cards was back in my sweaty, shaky, twenty-eight-year-old hands. Candy buys in, and I'm off to the majors; Candy doesn't, then it's back to the minors.

For the next two weeks I ate, slept, and breathed John Candy. I got hold of some tapes of his old TV show, *SCTV*; I rented *Volunteers*, *Splash*, *Spaceballs*, *Stripes*, and other cinema Candy; I saw *Planes, Trains and Automobiles* so many times I could mouth the dialogue by heart. In those pre-Internet days, I researched Candy by bribing my former newspaper colleagues who could keep a secret to raid their companies' archives. I condensed all of my knowledge and my pitch onto two single-spaced pages of yellow legal paper, and, on April 21, I boarded the plane that would deliver me to my destiny. Wanting to be in tip-top shape, I splurged on a business-class flight to L.A. Wanting to feed my brain, I chose the fish (instead of the beef or chicken) for lunch.

A brief aside. Are you familiar with "the chaos effect," in which, presumably, the flutter of a butterfly's wings in Borneo sets off a chain reaction that results in a stock market crash on Wall Street? Well, the fish lunch was my fluttering butterfly. Read on—you'll soon understand.

I'm not the best flier in the world, and the landing we made at LAX was particularly rough due to a heavy rainstorm in the Los Angeles area. "Great omen," I moaned as I got off the plane. I'd been given step-by-step instructions to get from the airport to Candy's place at 12328 Montana Avenue, but the pouring rain made it hard to see the street signs, and I got lost. These being pre-cell-phone days, too, I had to schlep from my car (a Toyota Supra convertible, which performed horribly on slick L.A. roads) to a pay phone to call Candy's assistant, Rosemary Chiaverini, for directions.

By the time I finally made it, I was about twenty minutes late (no big deal in a town where promptness is assumed to be a sign of weakness), stressed, and, shall we say, moist. Waiting for me were Marty and John. But they weren't alone. To further fray my already tattered nerves, the two had been joined by John's publicist, his lawyer, his accountant, and the omnipresent Rosemary. They all sat on one side of a massive dining room table; I faced them alone from the other side. "Christ, it's like *Judgment at Nuremberg*," I thought. To make matters worse, they all smoked. Positioned directly opposite them, I bore the brunt of each exhale. The left side of my skull started to pound, but I ignored the headache. The Tylenol would have to wait until after I'd won them over.

"Andy runs a great event," Marty beamed benevolently. "Tell us about it." I had broken down my pitch into ten sections, a modular approach that allowed me to jump from "Hosting Duties" to "Discussion of Television II" to "Personal Comfort," depending on the direction of the conversation. I preached for forty-five minutes straight, deftly handling questions and objections, but my audience, although polite, did not appear convinced. The headache got worse.

And then, just as I was outlining the show's minimal production timetable—I had streamlined it to fit John's film shooting schedule—the entire chain reacted at once. The throbbing. The stress. The wetness. The rocky flight. The billows of smoke. And the fish. Especially, the fish. The room started to spin. Oh no! I had to throw up!

Mustering every ounce of decorum I possessed, I smiled graciously and inquired (note that I did not "ask," I "inquired"), "Pardon me, but is there a washroom nearby?" Rosemary pointed down the hall. I gently pushed my chair away from the table, straightened my torso, and tenderly moseyed on down towards the promised land. I'll never forget the beautiful sound of the bathroom door clicking shut. Once safely ensconced behind it, I ripped open both faucets full blast. I knew I didn't have much time, so I power puked, spewing the bile from my gut with turbo force, trying my best to be discrete and quiet while doing it. "Way to go," I said to myself. "You've got your date with destiny, and you end up spending it with your head plunged deep inside John Candy's toilet."

After a few seconds I pulled my head out and pulled myself together. I cleaned the bowl and washed my face with cold water. Less than two minutes after leaving the table, I elegantly sauntered back to it.

Enter Andy.

"As I was saying," I remarked nonchalantly. I sat down and continued my pitch. Nobody had noticed anything out of the ordinary.

Or so I thought. When I glanced up from my notes, I saw six people staring at me, appalled. By the looks on their faces, you'd think they'd seen a ghost; apparently, the color of my face had led them to believe I was one. Candy immediately sprang into action. "Quick! Get him something to drink!" In an instant all six of them were running madly off in all directions. Rosemary brought a fizzing glass of Alka-Seltzer. Paul Flaherty, John's publicist, threw the windows open. Marty picked up my leather binder and started fanning me. When the action had died down and a semblance of tint had returned to my features, I tried to get the pitch back on track. "Forget it—put it away," Candy laughed. "I'll do it. I'll do whatever you want. I just don't want to be responsible for killing you."

For that I would have to wait a few weeks. Now, as I walked back to my car, blissfully impervious to the downpour, I had other things on my mind. I had a show to produce! The first step was a press blitz. After we promised them the scoop, the *Hollywood Reporter* rewarded us by announcing the HBO deal and the Candy signing on the front page of its May 3 edition. As expected, all of Canada got behind its native son and trumpeted his return home. More than just an entertainment story, the item made the national news and the front pages of newspapers from coast to coast. John posed with the festival's mascot for an

unforgettable publicity photo, which was picked up all over the continent after the festival's major press conference later in May. An ecstatic
HBO plastered Candy all over its July program guide and prepared an
extensive marketing campaign to hype the show. Kaminsky, Miller, and
their minions were in place. Tens of thousands of dollars were being
spent on the show every day. You want heat? This was a firestorm.

I began to enjoy a phenomenon called "stardom by association."
Ever since the Candy announcement, everywhere I went people rushed
over to me with their congratulations. Thursday, June 2 was no exception. After visiting a friend in the hospital and fielding umpteen ticket
requests from doctors, I met my wife, Lynn, and another couple for dinner at La Diligence, a local steakhouse. The restaurant's staff picked up
the tab for all four of us. "Thanks for putting the city on the map," they
said sincerely. In less than six months the festival had gone from boring
to boom. I ordered a drink, sat back, and relaxed, letting feelings of
accomplishment and contentment wash over me.

I enjoyed those feelings for an entire half hour. When we got home,
I casually asked the babysitter if anyone had called. "Your mother," she
replied. "Oh, and a guy named Marty Klein." Oh, jeez. Call me paranoid,
but after years in showbiz you develop a sixth sense; you just know
when the news ain't good. I had spoken to Marty almost daily since our
first encounter, but this was the first time he had ever called me at
home. I tore the paper with the message on it out of the babysitter's
hand and called Marty at home, also for the first time.

Marty Klein lived in an ultraswank condo complex just below Sunset Boulevard in Beverly Hills. Not only did his building have a doorman, but so did his phone. I'm sure clients like Steve Martin or Johnny
Cash had access to a private line, but I had to endure a wait of what
seemed like hours between the "doorman" asking who was calling and
then actually putting me through. Knowing it was me, Marty picked up
the phone already speaking.

"*That fat fuck! That fat fuck!*"

"Hello? Marty?"

"*That fat fuck! That fat fuck! That fat fuck!*"

"Marty? What's going on?"

"He's pulling out! *That fat fuck!*"

I hoped it would turn out to be some bad joke, or some sick initiation rite devised by a degenerate at HBO, but no such luck. I sank slowly to the kitchen floor, listening to Marty rail against his star client, and I saw my whole world come crashing down. "That piece of shit!" Marty fumed. "He always overcommits himself! Goddammit! I knew this would happen! *That fat fuck!*" If there was any consolation to this nightmare, it was hearing Marty's voice. Totally incongruent with his handsome features, it sounded somewhat like Kermit the Frog's (in fact, when Jim Henson died, Martin Mull—another devoted Marty Klein client—asked, "I wonder who's gonna do Marty's voice now?"). "This is surreal," I said to myself as I listened to Marty swear, curse, and threaten like a Muppet with Tourette's syndrome.

To avoid opening painful wounds that have long since been healed by time and therapy, let me just summarize the situation by saying that Candy felt overwhelmed by the number of days the TV show would take out of his schedule; he was in Vancouver shooting a film (*Who's Harry Crumb?*) that was running overtime, and he wanted out of the festival. Unfortunately, we were six weeks away from a live broadcast that had been widely announced and universally heralded. A no-show would not only severely wound the festival, but it would also kill the HBO deal, leaving us humiliated and substantially poorer.

We did have one last chance to ward off disaster, though. Once again, Marty managed to set up a tête-à-tête between yours truly and John Candy. This time, however, the meeting was one-on-one. Candy had to be on the set the following day at 9:00 A.M. Vancouver time. He was expecting me to call him at his hotel an hour earlier. Needless to say, I've had better nights of sleep than that of June 2, 1988. Once again, I prepared myself with reams of notes, which I'd scribbled on the back of a full-page festival newspaper ad featuring you know who. Looking back on the notes, I laugh at how unsophisticated some of my arguments were, including:

- I'm not here to reap guilt, but to suggest a way to satisfy all parties involved.
- The show is ready. The producer is ready. Your makeup and hair people are ready.

- You owe me nothing, but it's my career. I'm twenty-eight years old and this can kill it.

I wanted to find an appropriate motivational tune to pump me up on my drive in to the office, but in my exhausted state all I could find among my tapes was the Abba song "The Winner Takes It All," so I listened to the Swedish quartet warble it over and over. I wracked my brain to come up with something I could use to win Candy over this time. I couldn't puke again—that trick was old hat by now. I was seriously considering faxing over a picture of my wife and newborn son when the idea hit. At the time, the Just For Laughs offices were on the third floor of a building smack dab in the middle of one of the city's busiest pedestrian areas. Packed with restaurants, bars, and boutiques, Prince Arthur East was always noisy, and today, when I had yet another date with the devil of destiny, I would use the cacophony to my advantage.

At 10:57 A.M. Eastern time, I dialed Candy at La Residence in Vancouver, opened the window of Gilbert's office, and climbed out on the ledge. John answered, sounding hoarse and remorseful, but I wasn't going to let his puppy-dog manner get to me. "John, you hear all that noise? Well, I'm out on the ledge of my building, and if you don't agree to do the show, I'm gonna jump."

He laughed, but he wasn't going to be a pushover this time. He made excuses, but I countered each one. "I'm gonna urge, implore, and plead with you until you change your mind," I told him. By now, a crowd had gathered below me, and the clatter was increasing. At times, I could hardly make out what Candy was saying, but I plodded on, phone in one hand, notes in the other. Close to forty minutes later, I climbed back through the window breathing a big sigh of relief. Candy was back in. And, other than Marty Klein and my wife, nobody ever knew that he had pulled out. The worst was over. Or so I naively thought.

Enter John. Finally.

He arrived in the late afternoon on Wednesday, July 20, and he had to deliver the live HBO show on Saturday, July 23. Dress rehearsal was on Friday, and since he was already in town, John agreed to introduce twenty-five performers for our CBC series on Saturday for an additional $25,000. Quite a workload for three days, yet during both the puke and the ledge episodes, I had promised John that the festival experience would be equal parts work and vacation for him.[20] To live up to the vacation part of my pledge, we brought in eleven members of John's family[21] and booked a group of his Second City buddies to perform all week. In addition to the imported family and friends, Marty Klein was around, as were scores of other Hollywood types attracted for the first time to Just For Laughs by the Candy magnet. Surrounding him with familiarity proved to be another "fluttering butterfly."

It took about two hours for the festival to become Candy's kingdom. Starting Wednesday, he held court nightly in the far end of the Delta's Le Cordial, reminiscing, drinking, chain-smoking, and laughing with gusto.

John partied hard, but he worked hard, too. For this mega, live-TV event he would play a number of different characters, including a chain-festooned rapper and a stuffy government official named Gordon Massey-Ferguson. Friday night's dress rehearsal went fairly well, and we taped it as a safety measure, just in case anything screwed up with the live satellite feed on Saturday. Following Friday's show, the production staff and a handful of HBO execs gathered in the suite of Stu Smiley (HBO's VP of comedy programming) to watch the tape and make last-minute changes. It was almost 3:00 A.M. "Someone better make sure that Candy gets to bed," Smiley smirked.

As the newly minted executive producer of the show, I volunteered my services and made my way down to Le Cordial. Of course, there was John, trading war stories with *SCTV* vets Ron James and Robin Duke (also of *Saturday Night Live* fame). I had never seen him so happy. "Don't

---

[20] We provided him with a personal city guide, but the only landmark that interested John was the Montreal Forum, home of the legendary Canadiens hockey team. Although it was summer break, the team gave him a behind-the-scenes tour and thrilled him with a gift of an official Canadiens hockey sweater that had "CANDY" written across the shoulders.

[21] We had also promised him "the biggest suite in the city," and, as a practical joke, Gilbert had arranged for the Hyatt's grand ballroom to be converted into living quarters. There was a massive bed, a miniature movie theater, a fountain spewing Coca-Cola, exercise equipment, a mountain of toys for the kids, and two chauffeur-driven golf carts to get around the expansive "suite." John and his wife, Rose, caught on after a few minutes, but their kids were noticeably depressed with the move over to the more practical presidential suite of the Delta Hotel.

worry," he told me when I reminded him of the big show coming up. You know—the one that the whole country was counting on him to pull off. The one that would make my career. "One last drink, and I'll see you in the morning." Morning? "Aren't you coming to watch me record those CBC intros?" he asked. "Of course," I said. "What time?" He looked at his watch. "Oh about seven hours from now." I smiled uneasily. "Okay, see you there."

I was amazed to see John show up on time the next morning. Granted, he was tired, but he was chipper and ready to roll. A pro's a pro, I figured. For the next three hours he introduced performers who weren't there and made stage entrances talking to a nonexistent audience. By the time our CBC producers were finished editing this stuff, it would blend seamlessly with the performances taped throughout the week, but on this morning after the night before, John was alone, reading line after line in take after take. By 1:00 P.M. the fatigue was evident in his delivery, and there was an overabundance of throat clearing and "ahems," so Bob Kaminsky and Carol Reynolds, supervising the recording for the CBC, wrapped the session and sent John back to his dressing room. He had one hour to rest before final rehearsals started for that night's show.

The St. Denis Theater is a gorgeous old structure, but at that time its backstage amenities left a lot to be desired. To keep John cool between introductions and costume changes, we augmented the building's meager air-conditioning system with a primitive cooling method— a fan blowing on huge cakes of ice. Great for the skin, but not so wonderful for the throat. We kept this going throughout the afternoon rehearsal. We finished rehearsing just minutes before the theater doors were opened to the public. On with the show, this is it.

To ensure that the massive television audience would see a hot program, we scheduled a seventy-five-minute warm-up show prior to the live telecast. At ten minutes to 10:00 P.M., Paul Miller, a veteran of live TV, got on the mike to rile up the crowd. At ten seconds to 10:00, he started a countdown. The audience was already going berserk by the count of three. Then the curtain rose to reveal Leo Yoshimura's magnificent set (an eighteen-foot, spinning, opening-and-closing steamer trunk), an announcer's voice called out "Live from Montreal," the HBO opening montage appeared on the giant screen, and the crowd erupted in the type of ovation usually reserved for game-winning goals or home runs.

To intensify the frenzy, the show kicked off with a rap number by Barry Sobel. Starting from the back of the hall, Sobel snaked his way through the standing, clapping, chanting audience. As this was going on, John Candy—decked out in a porkpie hat, dark shades, and a mile of gold chain—was snuck onstage, and he stood in shadow before two turntables. While Sobel rapped, Candy's silhouette feigned some record scratching. Then, climbing onstage, Sobel performed his final verse.

I'd like to introduce a man who's fine and dandy
He ain't Barry Manilow, he won't sing "Mandy"
He's a stand-up kind of guy, a real Jim Dandy,
My favorite "Volunteer," Tom Hanks!
I kid . . . *John Candy!*

And, with that, every light in the theater fixed its beam upon the show's star. Candy was led to center stage by Sobel's backup singers. The band whipped itself into an orgy of high-pitched squeals and thumping bass. The crowd went nuts. This was the antithesis of the one man, one spotlight drudgery of the year before; it was world-class, eye-popping, ear-splitting entertainment excitement. What's more, the song-and-dance number symbolized our new beginning. The show opening was flowing along like a dream.

But then Candy delivered his opening lines: *"Hello Montreal! Are you ready to party?"*

They came out broken and croaky. *"I said, are you ready to party?"* Again, coarse and raspy.

And then came the straw that broke the camel's back—Candy's introduction of the night's first act, a one-man Jackson 5 impersonator (don't ask) named Christopher: *"Good, 'cause here he is! Christopher!"* There was no joy in Mudville. With the word "Christopher," Mighty Candy's voice shattered like a ten-cent lightbulb.

Once again, the fluttering butterfly had triggered chaos. Perhaps it was the noise level; Candy couldn't hear himself think, let alone speak

John Candy: the man saved my career,
but he almost killed me in the process.

(Kaminsky still blames the soundman, insisting that the monitors weren't cranked loud enough). Add to this John's nonstop partying, the cigarettes, the icy breeze from the fan, and the marathon CBC session earlier in the day. Whatever the cause, the result was obvious: John Candy had lost his voice. And, let's see, we still had fifty-eight minutes of TV to deliver. Live. To millions of homes across the U.S.A.

Candy came backstage with pure terror in his eyes. Christopher's musical bit would last only as long as the Jackson 5 tune "The Love You Save," which gave us about three minutes not only to restore our star's vocal chords, but also to get him out of his funky rap outfit and into his elegant host's tuxedo. Panic struck fast and hard. Smiley, an alarmist at best, added to the pandemonium by shouting, "Do we cut to the safety? Should we go to the safety?"

Like an army sergeant under enemy attack, Kaminsky barked orders:

"Get fucking tea! With honey!" And, within an instant, everyone back-stage—TV execs, hangers-on, technicians, even some of the performers scheduled to appear later in the show—had scattered and were racing through the streets of Montreal in search of hot beverages. I had no time to pace; I took off with the rest of them. Shortly afterwards, steaming cups filled just about every surface in the theater's dressing rooms, corridors, and wings (in fact, it was reminiscent of the scene in the musical *Phantom* where hundreds of tiny candle flames glow all over the stage—only in this case it was wisps of vapor all over the back-stage area).

Whenever Candy left the stage during the rest of the show, some-one would be waiting for him with a cup of hot tea. Not only is it a miracle that he made it through the hour delivering every line, but it's also amazing that he made it through without his bladder bursting. When he finally raised his arm and croaked, "You have been a wonder-ful, wonderful audience! Thank you, Montreal!" I breathed yet another massive sigh of relief. During that fateful "pull out" phone call with Marty Klein, I had moaned about how goddamn tough producing a TV show was. Marty had sternly replied, "If it were easy, then everyone would be doing it." Only now, as the audience rallied for yet another curtain call, did I fully appreciate the wisdom of his words.

Unfortunately, the next time I saw John Candy and Marty Klein together was at Marty's funeral. It was the fall of 1992. Before he even turned fifty, Marty died of a massive heart attack. His final send-off took place at Hillside Memorial Park, the lush cemetery where Al Jolson and other old-time Hollywood stars are buried. John—along with Johnny Cash (who sang "Amazing Grace") and Michael Fuchs—had been asked to eulogize Marty. Although he had moved on to another agency by then, John was heartbroken; he could hardly get a word out between anguished sobs.

John and I worked together at Just For Laughs again, when he agreed to host our 1993 Showtime show, but things weren't the same. Gone was the big, mischievous imp, and in his place was a puffy, sulk-ing hulk, beleaguered by too many business deals and a fading film presence. The incessant partying had given way to nonstop pressure. In 1988, John had left behind a handwritten note of thanks and a bottle of expensive champagne. In 1993 he wouldn't even open his dressing-room door to say goodbye after the show was over. Less than a year later I was saddened, but not shocked, when I heard that John, too, had succumbed to a massive coronary.

Way back on that morning when I spoke to John in Vancouver from my precarious perch on the office window ledge, I told him that if he consented to do my show, he'd have the country's appreciation and the festival's appreciation, but, most importantly, he'd also have the sincere appreciation of one man, forever. Wherever he may be now, I'd like him to know he still has it. For without John Candy, 1988 would've been just another year.

FIVE

WHAT HATH
I WROUGHT?

Although the primary function of Just For Laughs was to spread oodles of joy through its eight target markets (the three-word mission statement I instituted read, simply, "Make people happy"), there were times when my efforts went a little astray, and the results of my hard work were the opposite of what I'd intended.

Uh, let me put it another way, without the sugarcoating.

On many a night, after a particularly bad act or show, I went to bed feeling that Dr. Robert Oppenheimer was a kindred spirit; I understood how he must've felt the day the *Enola Gay* dropped its payload on Hiroshima. Seeking heavenly salvation, I would look to the skies, throw up my hands, and wail, "Oh Lord, what hath I wrought?"

To this, you must be saying, "Aw, c'mon. It's just a freakin' comedy festival, for Christ's sake. It couldn't be all that bad." Oh yeah? Let's see if you have the same opinion by the end of this chapter, after I've relived some of my darkest nightmares of comedic carnage for your amusement pleasure.

JERRY SADOWITZ

Taking risks was always a guiding principle behind Just For Laughs, but, in booking this Scottish magician-cum-comedian, we didn't merely push the envelope, we hacked it open with a rusty machete and sprinkled the dried glue from the flap on society's sense of decency. Them's fighting words—but that's actually what happened in 1991. Here's how it came about.

Two things you wouldn't realize upon first meeting the introverted, skinny, polite, and pleasant Jerry Sadowitz: one, he was among the world's most eminent close-up magicians; and two, he was the most foul-mouthed, aggressive, and uncontrollable comedian you'd ever come across. With his hooked nose and bowler hat, he was a Punch-and-Judy puppet come to life, and, with his nihilistic show called Total Abuse, he was upsetting the British comedy establishment in a manner unseen since Lenny Bruce blasted American comedy conventions in the sixties.[22] We knew we were taking a chance by putting this Glaswegian in a gala lineup, but with our X-rated club series The Nasty Show becoming the festival's most popular, Bruce Hills and I felt that it would be interesting to see how a controversial club performer would cross over to a big room.

Jerry was actually scheduled to appear on the Thursday, July 19 gala, but he was feeling a little under the weather. "His body's really having a hard time with the jet lag," his manager, Jon Thoday, explained. Aw, poor thing! So we moved him to Saturday to be part of the three-act warm-up for our prestigious Showtime show. We were worried that he still wouldn't be up to it by then, but when I saw Jerry walking around downtown, hand-in-hand with—get this—his mother and sister early on Saturday morning, I knew he'd be ready that night.

Ready? Boy, was he ready! "Hello moose fuckers!" was his salutation as he took to the stage. Within seconds of his walk-on we were already in too deep. Although Bruce had gone over Jerry's routine with him in advance, Jerry veered away from the approved material and zeroed in on a festering lesion—Quebec's volatile English-French political situation. He opened with, "Fifty percent of the people in this fucking country speak French, the other fifty percent let them get away with it. How do you fucking people stand for that? What's with all this

---

[22] Even wilder than his shows, where he would destroy his own props and set, was a weekly column he wrote in London's *Time Out* magazine. Dripping vitriol, he savagely attacked British showbiz icons, even going so far as to threaten to kill a few of them.

Jerry Sadowitz: polite and pleasant offstage, punched out onstage.

fucking French? You're not in France, you're in Canada!" He followed this with a few more jokes that were even less subtle.

The first line or two prompted a couple of scattered chuckles, but soon Sadowitz's ranting was being met with deafening silence. "Oh well," I said to myself, pacing slowly. "Chalk this one up to experience. In about a minute he'll be finished and this will all be forgotten." Wrong again, honey!

It was all too much for one of our faithful Francophone fans, forty-eight-year-old Bernard Fredette, and he left his seat in disgust. But, instead of heading to the lobby in search of a refund, he headed towards Jerry in search of blood. Most people thought it was all part of the act as they watched Fredette walk calmly up the access steps and onto the stage. Then things got ugly. Sadowitz was so focused on his tirade that he didn't even notice the intruder until Fredette leaned over his shoulder. After whispering something in Sadowitz's ear, Fredette proceeded to whack the shocked shock comedian in the face, pull him off the microphone, and ram him into the set's back wall.

At first, confusion. Except for the walls still undulating from the human collision, the stage was quiet. The audience buzzed, not entirely comprehending what had just happened. Then bedlam. Awakened from their slumber, the security guards joined Thoday in detaining the perpetrator and sequestering him from the angry backstage mob of festival people. And, finally, in the best P.T. Barnum tradition, we realized that the show must go on. Kevin Nealon, who had agreed to introduce the three warm-up acts, bounded onstage as if nothing unusual had happened. "Let's keep the show moving right along folks," he quipped, matter-of-factly. "Our next act . . ."

Fredette sat in a stairwell, smiling like Norman Bates in the final scene of *Psycho*, waiting for the police to come. A dazed Sadowitz was rushed to his dressing room. We sealed all backstage access doors to prevent more people from streaming in. Meanwhile, poor Brian Hartt was desperately trying to entertain the flabbergasted audience. (No wonder he gave up live performance soon afterwards to concentrate exclusively on comedy writing, becoming head writer for *The Kids in the Hall* and *MAD-TV*.) His attempt was a valiant one, but the damage had been already been done.

We took a brief intermission prior to the Showtime taping and spent it fighting off reporters, news cameras, and droves of curious onlookers. By the time Mary Tyler Moore took to the stage in her role as host, nobody in the room gave a damn about the show anymore (thank God it was only the dress rehearsal!); l'affaire Sadowitz was still on everyone's mind. Like Bobby Thompson's World Series–winning home run, the onstage whack became "The Shot Heard Around the World." It played big in the North American and overseas media, sparking weeks of debate on free-speech-versus-going-too-far in editorials, in letters to the editor, and on open-line shows.[23] Videotape of the assault became a popular bootleg.

And the players themselves? The last time I saw the radical Sadowitz was at the elegant Montreux Television Festival; he was being courted

---

[23] Fredette himself joined in the debate, writing an open letter to Jerry filled with self-righteous cop-outs like, "I meant no harm, only to signify my disapproval"; "I am not a violent man, but you left me no choice"; and, "I just want to speak the language of my ancestors who toiled this land for nearly four centuries."

at a tony lakeside terrace bar by British TV execs who wanted to sign him to a new series. As for Fredette, he went down swinging, retiring with an incredible batting average of 1.000.

THE PARADE

Surviving the Sadowitz escapade was tough, but it was a piece of cake compared to another Just For Laughs disaster that struck a mere four days earlier. This one started out harmlessly enough. To give our Showtime show a sense of the festival's extensive scope, producer Bob Kaminsky thought it would be fun to select some of our more interesting street performers and organize them into a parade. We would shoot the proceedings on Tuesday, July 16. The omnipresent Kevin Nealon, along with Jane Curtin (post-*Saturday Night Live* and pre-*Third Rock from the Sun*), would act as grand marshals and make semisnide remarks as the wacky acts passed by. Once edited, the parade would give us three-to-four minutes of good TV, a welcome breather from all the performance footage shot inside the theater. To assure that camera shots were unhampered by wandering humans, steel crowd-control barriers reminiscent of the Gulag were erected on both sides of the entire city block where the St. Denis Theater stands.

Naturally, a long fence, elaborate lighting, four cameras, and about seventy-five colorfully costumed entertainers will draw a crowd, and, an hour before the first performer was scheduled to walk along the route, the sidewalk space was already swarming. I perched high on a balcony overlooking the excitement, and, mike in hand, I served as the parade's public-address announcer, introducing each of the acts as they passed in front of the crowd.

The parade started without a hitch. Act after act, from inflatable man Fred Garbo to the safari-suited Kakal Band, strolled down the middle of the street to the delight of the swelling crowd. There were floats, as well, decorated mini-flatbeds pulled by golf carts and bearing everything from jugglers to festival mascot designer Vittorio Fiorucci, regally seated on a throne.

Remember the chaos effect—the fluttering butterfly that leads, via a chain reaction of small events, to a stock market crash? Well, on this evening, the butterfly was a guy named Stuart Feldman. Wearing an extremely goofy oversized foam cowboy hat, Stuart entered the parade route and began plying his trade—twisting balloons into doggies, or what have you. Much to his own amazement, apparently, the fenced-in hordes dug what he was doing, so, instead of moving along at the predetermined clip, Stuart stood still and played to an adoring portion of the crowd. The flow was interrupted. What had been a fluid, orderly line now stalled and zigzagged.

From my roost, I tried to rectify the situation using the loudspeakers.

"That was Stuart Feldman, ladies and gentlemen. Stuart Feldman," I said, courteously, but to no avail. I tried again.

"Let's hear it for Stuart Feldman as he moves along."

Still no reaction. I raised my voice to a bellow, bouncing it off the surrounding brownstones: "Stuart Feldman! Please move so that we can keep the parade coming!"

He remained oblivious. Finally, I dropped all hint of subtlety: *"Stuart Feldman! Move your fucking ass!"*

This last announcement did the trick, but, once again, the damage had been done. The rest of the procession was a tad off-kilter—no big deal, but the kerfuffle served to misalign the float carrying the parade's closing act, a combination one-man band and fireworks display named Remi Bricka.[24] As the final float lurched and stopped, lurched and stopped, its path drifted towards the west-side barricades. Because the entire march's timing was now in the toilet, Bricka's planned fireworks display detonated earlier than expected—again, no big deal . . . except that two of the rockets launched from the neck of his guitar flew over the barricades and into the crowd.

His flaming rockets were probably too strong for the occasion, but they would've fallen harmlessly on the cleared street had Bricka been centered. Instead, however, they were tearing through the shrieking, stampeding multitude. It was a cruel twist of fate that Bricka was cheerily strumming the Just For Laughs theme song when all hell broke loose. As I observed the rockets' red glare and the scattering people, I

---

[24] Trivia buffs may recognize the name, as Bricka holds a place in the *Guinness Book of World Records* for "Longest Walk on Water." Using a thirteen-foot-long pair of pontoon shoes, he slogged 3,502 miles from the Canary Islands to Trinidad between April 2 and May 31, 1988.

remember thinking, "Hmmm . . . now I know what it's like to be in Beirut."

Obviously, the parade was over. Some quick-thinking security guards threw down the barricades, averting further disaster, and people spilled onto the street. I was upset and slightly stunned by the experience, but, since everybody had dispersed and the situation had been defused so rapidly, I moved on to my next task of the evening—acting as MC for another outdoor TV shoot that Kaminsky had planned, this time within the safe, comfortable confines of the Air Canada stage.

As I made my way over there, I was intercepted by a hobbling, bleeding Brenda Branswell (now a reporter with *Maclean's*, Canada's national news magazine, but then one of my production assistants). She had tripped over a camera cable in her haste to get to me, and her leg looked like it had been caught in a meat grinder. "Oh my God! What happened to you?" I recoiled. "Never mind me," she panted, "wait 'til you see what's waiting for you in your office." On the run to the office Brenda explained that Bricka's fireworks had left some pretty ugly stains on two spectators—one of whom was an off-duty police officer, and both of whom were intent on speaking to me. I figured my MC duties would have to wait for a few minutes.

By the time I actually made it to my office—at this point a class-room in an old school we had converted—quite a mob had gathered. There was director Paul Miller, who had overseen the filming of the parade; my assistant, Robin Altman; the victims' families; and the victims themselves. One was completely topless, as a stray rocket had burned the shirt right off his back. The other was fully dressed, but he was holding onto his left ear, which looked like a piece of Chinese chicken soo guy dipped in cherry sauce. I don't recall my exact words, but I made some sort of lame joke to break the ice. It worked: the vic-tims smiled. "Robin, please get the man a T-shirt," I said, pointing her to our stash of festival merchandise. "Give him a sweatshirt, too. Clothes for everybody!"

When it was all over—after I'd dispensed my profuse apologies, bushels of Just For Laughs product, and a handful of tickets to the up-coming, sold-out Roseanne Barr show—the victims and their families left my office smiling. Pardon the pun, but yet another fire had been put out. We all breathed an intense sigh of relief. "Another satisfied customer," offered Robin, echoing a Just For Laughs client-service adage. "T-shirts and tickets," deadpanned the laconic Miller, shaking his head in disbelief. "You're lucky. If this were the States, they would own the festival by now."

GRAHAM CHAPMAN

As blasphemous as this might sound, one of the biggest letdowns in festival history was the legendary Graham Chapman's gala performance in 1987. I had booked one-fifth of Monty Python's Flying Circus for a solo show at Club Soda on July 18, a "stand-up lecture," as Graham called it, during which he would regale the audience with anecdotes, film clips, and Q&As. Even though the Monty Python group had broken up years before, its fans were still rabidly loyal; their deep devotion was more typical of the world of rock and roll than it was of comedy. Because of this, we felt that adding Graham to the bill of the July 17 gala would help boost ticket sales. Good business move. Bad artistic move.

We knew that Graham was not a stand-up comic, but he did assure us that there was enough stuff in his solo show to use for a seven-minute St. Denis Theater set. At rehearsal that Thursday afternoon he didn't actually rehearse, but he walked us through the seven minutes. He would wrestle with himself, tell a story or two, and move on to a demonstration of a pub game called "bum darts," which entailed picking up a quarter in his ass cheeks, waddling across the stage, and depositing the coin into a shot glass. Hmm . . . strange—but who was I to argue with a legend?

As he left the theater, Graham made a few inquiries about the city, including where he could obtain the freshest fish. Knowing he was on a very particular diet, I sent him to Waldman's, a Montreal fishmonger with a worldwide reputation. I even called ahead with the heads-up that Graham Chapman himself was coming over, "so please give him the best you have to offer." (How's that for excess? Requesting celebrity treatment at a fishmonger's!)

At the gala show, Graham was given a raucous reception. He walked onstage carrying an "I Love New York"–emblazoned plastic bag, hung it on the microphone stand, and bowed. As promised, he wrestled, spoke, and waddled, but the crowd was clearly nonplussed. I don't know what they were expecting—reenactments of Python classics, perhaps?—but this performance certainly wasn't it. Still, they showed respect for their icon and clapped graciously following each of his bits.

It was all a huge nonevent until the unscheduled, unrehearsed grand finale. As a parting shot, Graham reached into the plastic bag and calmly elucidated, "Now it's time to throw the fish." Flying circus? Try flying trout, tuna, and red snapper. Graham flung huge, full-bodied, slippery fish all over the theater. (Gotta give the guy credit, though— some of his tosses made it all the way up to the second balcony.) Now the audience went nuts. Like beach balls at a rock concert, the fish were bounced off to others as soon as they landed, lest someone be forced to share a seat with slimy seafood for the rest of the show. By the time the flounderstorm subsided, dozens of audience members were slathered in fish oil. Graham Chapman also gave new meaning to the term "stinking out the joint," as the barely air-conditioned theater was soon reeking of fetid fish.

The next day our offices were overrun with people demanding that we pay for their dry-cleaning or, worse yet, replace their ruined silk sweaters and dresses. Throughout all of this, Chapman remained unrepentant. "Be thankful," he told me, "that I didn't ask you to find me the best butcher."

BRIAN REGAN

The toughest job at a Just For Laughs gala was being the first night's first act. We called this slot "the wolverine," since it was like throwing a performer to the wolves. The holder of the wolverine slot carried all expectations of that year's festival on his or her shoulders; whoever we chose would be our lead-off batter, and the crowd expected a hit. Because of this, Bruce and I always made sure that we settled on a seasoned pro to handle the position.

In 1996 this pro was Brian Regan. A stand-up who had just won the Best Club Comic title at the American Comedy Awards, Brian had been through the rigors of hell gigs everywhere. He was one of the true good guys in the business, and we were happy and confident in giving him this responsibility. Brian was as sure a sure thing as you could get in the comedy industry.

Or at least he was until Wednesday, July 24. Perhaps the problem was that host Barry Humphries, in his Dame Edna Everage guise, was too strong. Maybe it was just an off night. Whatever the reason, Regan's performance (or performances) was about to become an indelible part of Just For Laughs lore. To a blast of music from the festival band, Brian walked onstage and did about a minute's worth of material that prompted a lukewarm, but entirely acceptable, reaction. But then, instead of plodding on, he did something never before seen at a festival gala. He asked to start over.

"You know, I-I-I've never done this before," confessed Brian, "but I kinda screwed up my opening thing, and I would like to start again. Do you mind? I know it sounds really stupid, and you're all going, 'What the hell's the matter with this guy,' but I want to do this again, all right?" He excused himself, returned to the wings, cued the band, and walked on again as if nothing had happened.

Take two. "It's good to be here!" Brian exclaimed. "Feels like I've been here before." Unfortunately, things didn't improve much for Brian the second time around. The audience didn't know how to react to a comedian taking a mulligan. What had been lukewarm now became hushed. Once more, Brian stopped.

"I'm gonna level with you," he pleaded. "This is a very important set for me, folks. I know you've heard the first two minutes. I'm gonna do it again, and if you could help me out and fake like crazy, that would help me tremendously. Thank you very much. I'll be out in about eight seconds." Backstage, witnessing all this on the monitors, we were as perplexed as the audience was. Either something was wrong, or Regan— the meat-and-potatoes comic—was taking creative liberties and engaging in some sort of avant-garde performance art. A total bust or a stroke of brilliance? We watched apprehensively.

Take three. Once more, the band played the walk-on music. Reaching center stage, Brian was greeted with rowdy applause. Smiling, he enthused, "It is great to be here!" There is an astute Chinese proverb that goes, "Be careful what you wish for, for it may come true." Brian suddenly found himself a living example of it. He had asked for the crowd's support, and now, surreally, he was getting it: every sentence, every clause, and every syllable was met with uproarious laughter and cheers. For an incredible third time in five minutes, Brian called a time out.

"I'm telling you, folks, this was not the kind of help I was looking for," he sighed, exasperated, before giving the crowd a brief introduction to Comedy 101. "I know this sounds really messed up, but if you could laugh at the punchlines and not at the setups? Folks, my career is in your hands. I'm gonna do some setups. You can just sit there and watch during those. And then when the punchlines come, if you could laugh then, I would appreciate it." And with that, Brian was off again.

Backstage, it had become evident that none of this was intentional. Something had gone wrong. Very wrong. Bruce Hills was flipping out—pacing and babbling, "What's he doing out there? I'm gonna kill him! Where's Rory [Rosegarten, Brian's manager]?"[25]

Take four.

You know the routine by now. Band. Walk-on. Center stage. Applause. Brian removed the microphone from its stand, surveyed the room, and beamed. "Nice crowd!" he said, in all sincerity. This time he actually went through with it. Good thing, too, as Bruce was waiting to tackle him and send out the next act had Brian returned to the wings thinking he'd take a fifth kick at the can.

Needless to say, Brian's wolverine turn had the festival howling; it overshadowed every other highlight that year.[26] Brian apologized to us; and, since he was such a nice guy, we couldn't hold it against him. Still, when he made a return visit to Just For Laughs in 1999, we played it safe. We scheduled him in the second half of a weekend gala and then held our collective breath until we heard him utter the closing words, "Thank you! Goodnight!"

---

[25] Two years earlier Bruce and Rory had been through a similar nightmare when Dick Cavett, another Rosegarten client, took close to half an hour to complete a screwed-up seven-minute magic trick.

[26] Although it was kind of cruel, one of the funniest reactions to the Regan incident was a review of the show in the daily *Newsrag*, an "insider" publication written by festival comics. The review stopped and restarted four times.

EDDY WINDSOR

Eddy was a dog act, and, as you can assume from his inclusion in this section, the description can be taken two ways. Although he appeared way back in 1987, Eddy's legend lives on, so much so that he was voted "Worst Act of All Time" by festival aficionados.

He was born into one of Europe's leading circus families, one that had been training animals of all types—from elephants to dolphins to horses—for six generations. I sincerely hope that Eddy had better luck with those more dangerous creatures than he had with Miss Lolo Bassett, the lumbering, sad-eyed canine he brought to Just For Laughs.

Thankfully, I can take no responsibility for this debacle. Eddy was booked sight unseen by Alain Cousineau, the festival's general manager, in '87, on a tip from a France-based talent agent named Monique Nakachian. Eddy was slaying 'em down at the Moulin Rouge, and with credits from everywhere—*The Ed Sullivan Show* to Las Vegas—he seemed like a fine addition to our growing festival's lineup. In fact, to allow Eddy to fulfill his weeklong Just For Laughs commitment, Sammy Davis Jr. himself had let him out of a Vegas contract where Eddy was Davis's opening act. Now that's impressive!

Less impressive was Eddy's performance. It went beyond the realm of tacky. A derby-wearing, umbrella-swinging Windsor came onstage alone, engaged the audience in some chitchat, and then called for his "sexy" assistant—the aforementioned mutt. Then, inspiring either sheer boredom or utter revulsion in the crowd, Eddy and Lolo would perform some inane stunts—or fail to perform them. I still don't know whether it was all part of the act, but Lolo just couldn't do what Massah Eddy was asking of her.

On Friday, July 10, the polygot Eddy did his bit as part of a French-language gala. Poor Lolo was as responsive as a slug; a condition Eddy blamed on her inability to understand French. Following the show, stage director Jean Bissonnette ran to me to report that he'd heard squeals emanating from the duo's dressing room. "Holy shit!" he said in dismay, "I think he's beating the dog." Not surprisingly, things didn't go much better a week later when Eddy performed in English, Lolo's mother tongue.

As dreadful as this was, the real pain was only felt a few weeks later. By now Eddy's act had taken on mythical status, and we were inundated with insider requests to see it. Reviewing the tapes of Eddy's performance, Bruce Hills stumbled upon footage from an unseen "Iso," an isolated camera that, for editing purposes, shoots close-ups and angles the main cameras don't capture. For some strange reason, the Iso camera was focused on Miss Lolo's backside, and it revealed a trade secret: as a cue for a trick in which Lolo would rise as Eddy cranked her tale like a car jack, Eddy would stick his finger inside the dog's ass! Those we showed this tape to either ran from the room repulsed or collapsed, weak-kneed, with laughter.

They do say, though, that every cloud has a silver lining. Because of Eddy we developed an important new policy: unless one of us had seen an act either live or on tape, it would never appear on a Just For Laughs stage.

MR. METHANE

Even with the Windsor Rule in place, we still made our share of blunders. But the one that blows all others away was my booking of Paul Oldfield in 1994. A lanky, timid Englishman in real life, Paul would don a lime-green leotard with a huge M on the chest, drape a flowing cape over his shoulders, and cover his eyes with a cheap green mask to become Mr. Methane, flatulence king of the universe!

As vulgar and lowbrow as it sounds, I had been searching for a fart act ever since I'd read about Joseph Pujol, a French baker better known as Le Petomane (literally, "The Fartmaniac"). His act consisted of playing music, blowing out candles, projecting darts, and doing impressions of famous politicians using only his sphincter and its pipeline of natural gas. More than just a freakish curiosity, Le Petomane was, in his prime, one of Europe's most popular mainstream entertainers, earning more money than the divine Miss Sarah Bernhardt did in the 1890s.

When I—how shall I put it?—got wind of Mr. Methane, I acted fast; I wasn't going to let this opportunity pass me by. Not only did I book him for the festival, but I also gave him a prominent spot on our live Showtime broadcast, that year hosted by two of television's biggest stars, the dynamic duo of Kelsey Grammer and Brett Butler.

Mr. Methane filling the gas tank. How subtle . . .

Simultaneously impressive and nauseating, Mr. Methane's act didn't deviate much from his predecessor's, performed a century earlier. He joined our tuxedoed bandleader, Scott Price, in a piano/anus duet of Strauss's "Blue Danube Waltz" and blew out the candles on a birthday cake, among other stunts. Yet somehow the audience didn't appreciate the historical and cultural elements of the performance. While most of the men laughed a bit, every woman in the St. Denis Theater that night—without exception—was unspeakably offended and stared down her male companion until he, too, went silent. This was hard enough for me to endure at the Friday night dress-rehearsal show, so, during the Saturday taping, I watched Mr. Methane's act from the privacy of the theater's roof-level offices, pacing with my eyes closed and my fingers in my ears, waiting for the vibration of the band's play-off from below as a signal for me to reappear downstairs.

To add to my torment, the scent of Mr. Methane wouldn't fade away easily. Of all the horrified women in attendance that night, none was more so than Bea Arthur, the tough-as-nails star of *Maude* and *Golden Girls*. Bea was in town to headline a spoken-word AIDS fundraiser we had put together for the following day, and, of course, we'd offered her front-row seats for the Showtime show. Like a heat-seeking missile, she flew backstage when it was all over to find the responsible party. Her first target was Bruce Hills, but, given his history with the Queen Bea,[27] he folded like an accordion and gave me up.

"Uh, uh, I didn't book him!" wavered Bruce. "Well, *who did?*" Bea growled. When Bruce replied, "It was Andy Nulman!" Bea tracked me down like a smart bomb (an impressive feat, due to the fact that I knew she was on the warpath and did my best to avoid a confrontation). When she finally struck, she did so with full force, lambasting me for my lack of taste in front of a crowd at the Delta Hotel.

---

[27] Unbeknownst to her, Bea was the source of a summerlong practical joke we pulled on Bruce. During a phone conversation, Bea had traumatized him by responding to his request for a press bio by bellowing, as only Bea Arthur can, "Bio? Bio? I'm Bea Arthur! *I'm Bea Arthur!*" Bruce had emerged from the experience pale and quivering. From that point on, whenever Bruce was away from his office, one of us would get on the intercom and say, "Bruce Hills: Bea Arthur on line 2," just to see him bolt to the nearest phone like a bat out of hell.

As soon as she left, Paul Oldfield strolled by, totally unrecognizable in his street clothes. "I hope I did okay for you tonight," he said respectfully. "Fine, fine," I responded, forcing a smile. And then Paul's face lit up. "Oh my gosh, isn't that Bea Arthur over there?" he asked. "Yeah," I replied, as I headed off the other way. "Why don't you go over and introduce yourself?"

WOODY BOP MUDDY

As traumatic as the Mr. Methane experience was, its final toll was merely a blow to my ego. Some mistakes are a little more costly. Take, for example, the case of Woody Bop Muddy, "The Demonic Disc Jockey." I was turned on to Woody by the late Pete Brown, a great British friend of mine who once managed the rock band Queen. Pete and I had a lot in common, most notably rock music, comedy, and fine English beer. On a cold November night in 1993, all three came together when Pete dragged me to a show at a London school assembly room. The assembled acts ran the gamut—from leftist stand-up acts to a senior-citizen ventriloquist whose dummy drove her to tears by taunting her about being old, ugly, and fat. Calling Dr. Freud!

But the man we were there specifically to see was the show's closer, and, after seeing Woody Bop Muddy, I immediately understood why. Dressed in a wildly checkered suit, sporting a Mohawk-with-tail haircut, Woody presented an act that involved a turntable, a bunch of old records, and a wooden post. After spinning a few seconds of insipid music—provided by the likes of Donny Osmond, The Bay City Rollers, Barry Manilow, or Kylie Minogue—Woody would poll the audience. A positive vote meant that the record would survive to be played at another show; a negative one would ensure that it was sent to the "record graveyard."

Naturally, the audience wanted a massacre, so just about every record Woody played met its death. But, ever the artist, Woody had a myriad of methods to send discs to their doom. He would nail them to the post, he would squirt them with lighter fluid and ignite them, he would stomp them with his Doc Martens, he would scratch them with the turntable needle until the crowd's ears practically bled. And, like a demented leprechaun, Woody would celebrate each act of destruction

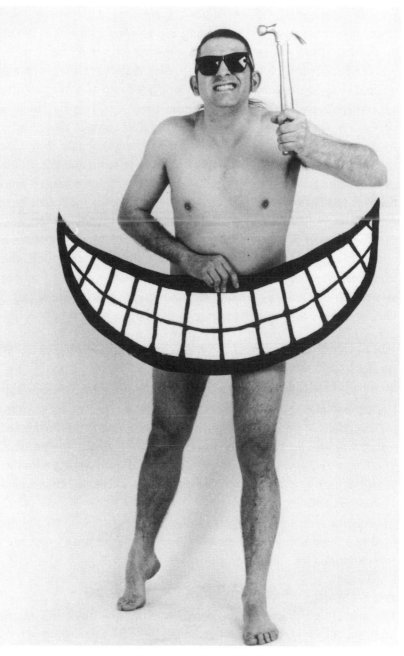

Woody Bop Muddy: he lost his clothes;
I lost a multimillion-dollar contract.

with his patented jig. This was a sick act, and I loved it. Perhaps it was the beer, perhaps it was Pete's goading, but I signed a suspicious Woody on the spot. ("Are you serious or just screwing with me?" he asked.)

Cut to Montreal, July 1994. Even I knew Woody wasn't gala material, but I was so high on this nut that I included him as part of another special we were filming for Showtime that year. This one he'd be perfect for. The Cutting Edge was an alternative comedy show hosted by Dom Irrera at Club Soda. In contrast to the glitzy gala shows, we tried to make this one raw. But there's raw as in sushi and there's raw as in festering carcass; unfortunately, The Cutting Edge leaned more towards the latter definition.

Our relationship with Showtime was already tenuous at this juncture (we were in the last year of a three-year deal with no guarantee of renewal), and the fact that our security staff, stung by accusations that they'd allowed overcrowding at the club, chose this night to demonstrate their efficiency by keeping certain network executives waiting in line for their own taping certainly didn't help matters. By the time Steve Hewitt, the Showtime VP in charge of making the final contract decision, squeezed his way through Club Soda's doors, guess which act was onstage?

It wasn't Woody's fault; he was just doing what he did best, but Hewitt was pissed off and totally unimpressed. "For this I'm paying a million dollars?" he kept asking anyone who would listen. In the end, his answer was no. Woody Bop Muddy's record graveyard had claimed another casualty—my Showtime contract. And until we signed a five-year deal with CBC years later, Just For Laughs never saw that type of TV money again.

Looking over my old tapes, I still get a laugh out of Woody Bop Muddy. Imagine how much more I'd enjoy him if he hadn't cost me a few million bucks.

THE WEDDING

The year 1989 was a rough one. Three gala hosts—Paul Reiser, Martin Mull, and Richard Lewis—canceled on us. This cast a pall over the festival. The media reported each cancelation with glee, insinuating, in the process, that the event's best days were over. To counterbalance this pessimism, I had to do two things: find replacement hosts and come up with something positive to deflect media criticism. I achieved step one within days. The idea I needed to achieve step two fell into my lap within hours.

Local scat singer/comedian E.J. Brulé always had some sort of off-the-wall scheme to promote. For once I was prepared to buy into one of them. E.J. was taking a bride, and he was looking for a unique way to celebrate their union. "Why not get married right on our stage?" I pitched. "It worked for Tiny Tim on *The Tonight Show* twenty years ago—it can work for you today!" No novice when it came to self-promotion, E.J. jumped on the concept. All he had to do was convince his bride to be. All I had to do was convince the media I wasn't kidding. "What could be more positive than a wedding?" I told them. "Publicity stunt!" they cried. "It's fully legit," I countered. "Come see for yourself."

E.J.'s wedding, which would take place after a gala show, became the theme of the evening. Replacement host Alan Thicke integrated it into his opening monologue, and, throughout the gala, assorted members of the clergy (actors, really) were ushered backstage. In addition, journalist Matthew Cope set up shop in the dressing rooms, interviewing E.J., his bride, her parents, and various relatives between acts. After a while, though, it all became too much for those involved. E.J. kept asking when the show was going to end. The acts on the gala roster were fed up with having to wait through Cope's interview segments. The audience thought the whole wedding stunt was cute, but they were more interested in the next gala performer than the size of the best man's shoes. They started booing Cope, and each time he reappeared they expressed their disapproval more heartily.

Once the final act had said his goodnight, Thicke introduced the actual minister, and the St. Denis Theater became a massive wedding chapel. Regrettably, many audience members didn't believe that this hallowed event was legitimate, and they got up to leave, bumping into the gown-and-tux-clad wedding participants, who were marching solemnly down the aisle in the opposite direction.

The gala acts wanted to kill me for drawing things out and screwing up the show's rhythm; CBC's Carol Reynolds, like Queen Victoria, declared, "We are not amused." But, despite the criticism and the initial skepticism, newspapers all over the world picked up the story and the accompanying photos. E.J. Brulé was no superstar, but at least his nuptials added some positive vibes to what could've been a downer year—so there!

GALA 5

I've saved the worst for last. No, not a single artist, but a whole show so entirely awful that it caused a public uprising. There's scraping the bottom of the barrel, and then there's breaking through to the floor below; that's what happened during the now-infamous Gala 5, which took place on Monday, July 25, 1994. It was a show that sank so fast and so low that it made the *Titanic* disaster look like a bathtub dunk.

What exacerbated matters was a build-up that raised expectations to stratospheric heights. For months we had been gushing over Marc de Hollogne, a so-called artistic genius from Belgium. Earlier on, Marc had appeared at Juste Pour Rire as a performer. This year we gave him the keys to daddy's expensive car: the closing French-language gala. Marc wouldn't just be starring in the show; he'd write and direct it, as well.

Like the mad scientist whose underground lab is off limits to everyone but himself, de Hollogne hatched his secret plans for this most unique show. He was determined, for one thing, to smash to smithereens the festival's antediluvian tradition of hosts introducing comedians. While he wouldn't share his ideas with any of us, de Hollogne did manage to play the coquette by screening the prerecorded video segments of the show—hallucinatory sequences featuring Pierre Richard, one of France's top film stars. We came. We saw. We conked out.

Yet, with so much riding on Gala 5, we shoved the show down media throats like chicken feed. We bought an unprecedented number of full-page ads. Marc did dozens of interviews to stoke the hype machine and drive the somewhat sluggish ticket sales. Backstage at the St. Denis Theater on that fateful afternoon, I ran into Jango Edwards. After two triumphant appearances at Just For Laughs, Jango was back exclusively for this extravaganza. "You won't believe this," he told me while humping my leg, "but we still haven't rehearsed yet." Yeah, right. And you have land for me in Florida. That Jango, such a kidder.

But when I returned to the theater that evening, the song remained the same. Faces in the dressing-room corridor were long and confused. Jango had dropped all wackiness; I could see fear in his baby blues. "I'm telling you, man, still no rehearsal," he whispered. Ever the cheerleader, though, he broke away from me and ran down the hall, yelling into each open door, "Rehearsal starts at six!" It was now 6:30 P.M. The show was to begin in an hour, but this one was gonna be late.

At 8:00 P.M., seconds before I would join 2,300 unsuspecting martyrs inside the St. Denis Theater, my cell phone rang. It was Elizabeth Roy, one of our publicists, asking if I'd shoot over to our outdoor site at Montreal's Old Port for an interview with Doris Synett, a top TV journalist "No can do," I told her. "I have to show support to Marc. I'm staying here." After twenty minutes of witnessing an aimless and painful spectacle, I called Elizabeth back. "I've reconsidered."

Etiquette obliged me to turn off my cell for the lengthy interview, but I turned it back on as soon as Doris had given me a goodbye handshake. Before the device could kick in fully, it rang one of those telltale rings of strife. It was Carole Hooper, our director of communications. I could barely hear her over the background clatter. "Where are you?" she screeched. "Where am I? Where are you?" I shouted back. It sounded as if she were in the midst of the Dresden bombing. "I'm in the box office," she yelled. "There's a riot . . ." And then the line went dead.

I rushed back to the theater in time to see hundreds of irate people storming the ticket wickets, besieging the handful of employees on duty. They banged on the glass with their fists, demanding both refunds and the scalps of those responsible. For a few minutes I actually considered calling in the riot squad to put an end to the uprising with a water-cannon blast or two.

The misguided masterpiece had been so bad that the audience had booed the performers off the stage. The show's title, L'Homme Ne Rit Plus ("Man No Longer Laughs"), was pathetically prophetic. Marc had opened the proceedings by appearing as a white-faced Pierrot clown. Among the performances that followed were a French group that manipulated black-face minstrel-show puppets while singing "Old Man River" (which ended up being pronounced "Old Man Weaver") and Jango, in his catastrophic festival swansong, as a ballerina dancing a tragic "Swan Lake." By the time Jango reappeared in a redneck outfit, dousing himself with beer and singing "Six Pack Blues," the outraged audience had seen enough. They booed so vociferously that de Hollogne had to reappear as Pierrot to give Jango the hook and mercifully pull the plug on the show.

The human hedge that surrounded the box office was too thick for me to penetrate, so I called Carole back on her cell phone. It was time for damage control. "As long as they have a ticket stub, give them their money back," was the directive. "No questions asked." Until the next morning, that is, when the media swooped down on this sitting duck of a story. In all fairness, they had been there to help build it up, and now they were here to help pull it down. In an attempt to add a bit of levity to the situation, I gave interviews from under my desk. But, really, what was there to say? We tried something and it didn't work. We're sorry, and we'll pay the price. We offered anyone who hadn't made a claim the night before the choice of a refund or a whole series of tickets to the 1995 festival. (Demonstrating their faith in us, most people chose the ticket package.)

Amazingly, some people didn't bother to take us up on our offer. Even more amazingly, some masochistically inclined types called us up to express their disappointment at having missed the gala. "I always wanted to be at one of those shows so bad that people get booed off the stage," said one. "I would've loved to experience it." Trust me, you wouldn't have.

Oh, and the answer to the question on everyone's mind: he's become a big-time movie star in Europe. Marc de Hollogne, that is. But, for some strange reason, he now goes by the name Marc Hollogne. Seems that Gala 5 tore a strip off him, too.

ALL CHOKED UP: JERRY LEWIS

To this day, every time I hear the words "Jerry Lewis," the right side of my face breaks out in an uncontrollable twitch. More than any other performer who's appeared at Just For Laughs, this comedy God wreaked havoc with my psyche. The stories of our encounters have become legendary, and incredulous friends insist that I tell them over and over.

First off, Jerry is a brilliant man. At one time, along with partner Dean Martin, he was the world's most popular performer. During his days as a solo star, he out-Carreyed Jim Carrey with his inimitable brand of uninhibited lunacy. His turn as an arrogant talk-show host opposite Robert De Niro in *The King of Comedy* ranks among my favorite film performances of all time. Offscreen, he is a successful writer and director. He is also the inventor of a number of technical processes, including Video Assist, a groundbreaking film/video synchronization system that allows filmmakers to screen and review their work immediately. Leading the annual Muscular Dystrophy Telethon, Lewis has raised millions of dollars for the fight against a debilitating childhood disease.

He also has, shall we say, a "reputation."

I couldn't wait to meet the man when he made his debut Just For Laughs appearance in 1986. Our paths didn't cross often that year, but the two times they did were classics. The first was backstage at the St. Denis Theater on July 17. Jerry was booked to headline his own, full-blown, twenty-piece-orchestra show at Place des Arts, but, for a few thousand dollars more, he also agreed to make an unannounced appearance at a gala show the next day. We only did three galas that year, each of them hosted by Andrea Martin, and while the *SCTV* vet was wonderful with a script, she had no stand-up or ad-lib experience. We feared she'd be overshadowed by such an imposing comedic presence as he walked onstage. Then someone came up with the idea of giving her one line to work with. She'd look down at herself, look at Jerry, and then say, "Finally! The reunion of Martin and Lewis!"

So, there we were, backstage on an oppressively hot July night, and gala producer Cynthia Grech was busy outlining the aforementioned comedic gem to Jerry. Everyone else was in various stages of undress to beat the heat, but Jerry stood calmly in a red polo shirt and a black Member's Only windbreaker. Although his mane glistened with trademark Jerry Lewis pomade, not a bead of sweat disturbed his brow. He nodded calmly as Grech once again explained how he should be positioned for Andrea to deliver her one and only line. From that point on, he could do and say whatever he wanted.

Minutes later, Jerry was introduced and treated to an ovation best described as "pleasant." While polite, the cheer that went up was far from tumultuous—perhaps a reflection on his Place des Arts show the night before. To anyone who had ever seen Jerry in Vegas, this solo show held no surprises, and it came off as somewhat archaic to the Montreal media; local scribes were accustomed to the alternative comedy of Just For Laughs. Rightfully or wrongfully, the show was savaged by reviewer Lucinda Chodan in that morning's Montreal *Gazette*. But more on her later.

Andrea Martin, amazingly perky given the sauna-like conditions, simulated shock as Jerry made his way onstage. She positioned herself perfectly, and, just as she was about to deliver her line, Jerry blurted, "Finally! The reunion of Martin and Lewis!" We were stunned. Whether Jerry had forgotten the producer's instructions or had simply stolen the line, we'll never know. As expected, the audience ate it up, but Andrea was left in the lurch. Clutching at straws, she started talking about the weather. After exchanging banalities with Jerry about the heat, Andrea, for some inexplicable reason, pulled open her top and asked Jerry to blow

down her cleavage. Jerry took an extended gander at her boobettes, lifted his head, and said, "I'd be afraid to lose what you got." Neil Simon banter it wasn't. After some more polite applause, Lewis left and the gala continued awkwardly. We all avoided eye contact as Jerry passed through the backstage area. Nobody knew what to say.

The following day we were once again rendered speechless by Jerry. The scene was a ballroom in the Hotel du Parc, set up to accommodate a Muscular Dystrophy Association press conference, Jerry's final commitment on his visit to Montreal. On one side of the dais were Roy Bonisteel and Michel Louvain, two MDA spokesmen; on the other were Gilbert and myself. In the middle, again wearing Member's Only, was Jerry. The press conference started innocently enough. MDA reps lauded Jerry for his exemplary work, and we thanked him for gracing us with his presence—the standard blah-blah. And then the fun began. Questions from the floor.

To be frank, I don't remember any of the queries posed that day except the one that detonated the explosion. A reporter referred to Chodan's scathing critique and asked Jerry if reviews still mattered to him after so many years in the business. Jerry began to answer very graciously, intelligently explaining the balance between the fragility of artists' hearts and the rhinoceros-like toughness of their skin. But then, as a coda, he took a potshot at the offending review: "You can't accept one individual's opinion, particularly if it's a female, and, you know— God willing, I hope for her sake it's not the case—but when they get a period, it's really difficult for them to function as normal human beings." Within milliseconds, all the air had been sucked out of the ballroom. A hush descended, soon followed by a fog of murmuring.

A quick aside. A press lensman captured this moment for posterity in a classic photograph—like the unforgettable images of American soldiers planting the flag at Iwo Jima or Lee Harvey Oswald being gunned down by Jack Ruby. In it, we see a teeth-gritting, laser-beam-eyed Jerry, fingers balled into a fist, spewing out his infamous words. Gilbert looks on shell-shocked, and I'm turning away, smirking nervously. A masterpiece!

Shortly after Jerry uttered his words, a female journalist jumped up to defend her gender. "Mr. Lewis!" she cried indignantly. "Shall we

The infamous 1986 MDA press conference: Jerry spits venom,
leaving Gilbert (second from left) shell-shocked and
me (far left) smirking nervously.

interpret a comment like that to mean that you have something
against women?" Lewis smiled. "Not with my sex drive, honey!"

The press conference broke up quickly, probably because the jour-
nalists present knew that they couldn't have dreamed up anything
more exciting than what they had just witnessed. They flew back to
their respective media outlets and gleefully got down to work. Sheep-
ishly, I approached Joe Stabile, Jerry's longtime manager and confidant.

"Will this affect him in any way?" I asked. "Oh, that Jerry," Stabile
replied in a manner that assured me he'd been in worse situations than
this. "Always saying these silly things!"

The incident became a cause célèbre throughout the North American media. Women's groups denounced Jerry. There were calls for him
to apologize, even to step down from his MDA responsibilities. But Jerry
is one tough customer. He rode out the storm, and by the time his tele-

thon hit the airwaves, about five weeks later, he'd managed to put the whole episode safely behind him.

But his legend lingered long at Just For Laughs, and "the incident" was the first thing brought up when we considered inviting him back to be part of our tenth anniversary celebrations in 1992. By now Lucinda Chodan had become the *Gazette's* entertainment editor, so, whatever plans we had for Jerry, we didn't count on much in the way of support from her. (To Lucinda's credit, after becoming an unwilling poster child for the women's movement in '86, she had too much class to even think about revenge in '92.)

Still, the festival needed to follow up the 1991 induction of Milton Berle to its Humor Hall of Fame with another icon, and Jerry certainly fit the bill. Another inducement to invite Jerry was the fact that the festival's tenth birthday coincided with the 350th anniversary of the city of Montreal, and to help celebrate it Gilbert had procured a whole whack of government cash to put together a show called The Just For Laughs 350th Symphony. Conceived and directed by former Cirque du Soleil director Guy Caron, the symphony would unite nonverbal, musical comedians from all over the globe who would perform their routines backed by the world-renowned I Musici orchestra. (To promote it, our crack PR team came up with lines like, "Roll over Beethoven and back down, Bach"; "Our symphony puts the emphasis on 'funny'"; and, "Juggling, painting, singing, and tumbling, mixed with awe-inspiring orchestration.") Although we only asked him to perform his ageless "musical typewriter" chestnut, we billed Jerry as the concert's headliner.

It was mid-March when I renewed my acquaintance with Joe Stabile. A veritable gentleman, he'd either forgotten the 1986 incident or he chose to ignore it, preferring to discuss how much fun he'd had at Just For Laughs. On March 27,[28] I spent the afternoon in my hotel room at L.A.'s Chateau Marmont banging out an offer to him so that we could once more work with Jerry Lewis. It was June before we had ironed out all the details, but the end result was that, for a fee that hovered around six figures, Jerry would accept Humor Hall of Fame

---

[28] The date is noteworthy, as it was the last time I would ever use a typewriter to compose anything.

awards in French on August 6, in English on August 9 (as part of our Showtime show), and deliver three performances taped for TV (these last three words are of great consequence; keep them in mind for later) as part of The Just For Laughs 350th Symphony on August 7 and 8.

On Wednesday, August 5, with visions of the aloof, nasty, vindictive character I'd encountered in 1986 filling my head, I reluctantly climbed into the limo that was to collect Jerry Lewis at the airport. Six years previously I had little to do with him other than watch, amused and intimidated, from the sidelines. This time around, as deal maker, festival head, and TV show executive producer, I was directly in the line of fire.

I shuddered when I caught sight of Jerry coming through the arrival doors. Press reports said that he had mellowed since the birth of his daughter, Danielle, and I figured that bringing along a gift for the baby would be a good icebreaker. Well the press was right, and so was I. He greeted me with a wild yelp and Lewisian facial contortion. From the moment we closed the limo door, he raved about his baby girl, showed me pictures, and recounted proud-papa tales, stopping only to praise Lily Tomlin (host of our Showtime TV show that year) for her role oppo-site Tom Waits in Robert Altman's *Short Cuts*. I took Jerry to the Four Seasons Hotel, introduced him to assistant Raemona Slodovnick (a moonlighting veterinarian whose expertise with animals made her the obvious choice to take care of our big stars every year), and bid him a cheery adieu. See you tomorrow, Jerr! Oh my God! He was a changed man! This was going to be a breeze.

Yeah. When will I learn?

Jerry's rehearsal began at Place des Arts at 1:00 P.M. At 1:10 I got my first phone call from Raemona. "You better get over here fast," she whispered. "He's really pissed off!" Oh, Christ. I zoomed out of the Delta Hotel like a maniac, driving the wrong way down a one-way street to get to the concert hall faster. Arriving there, I encountered a flurry of fury. "You little prick! A Lincoln town car? That's the type of car you send over for a movie star and director? A Lincoln town car? Where's my limo?" Although the words were loud, they were said with a smile, so my response was semiserious.

"Aw, come on, Jerr," I smiled back, "The contract said a car on call twenty-four hours. It's a simple screwup by our logistics department. If you really want a limo, I'll have one over here by the time you finish rehearsal." Still smiling, Lewis said, "That's what I want." Then he put his arm around my shoulder and squeezed. "A Lincoln town car! What were you thinking, you putz? You'd put a world-famous star in a Lincoln town car?" I extracted myself from his grip and called Claude Lemay, our logistics coordinator. "Five days of twenty-four-hour limo? It's not in our budget," he protested. "I don't care," I replied. "I want to live."

Another fire put out. I breathed a big sigh and reached for my car keys. They were gone. Fearing the worst, I ran outside and confirmed it: I'd been in such a terrorized rush to get to Jerry that I'd left the car running with the keys inside. In a no-parking zone! Good thing I was conscientious and locked the car doors, or someone could've driven off with it. So, there I sat, on the curb of a busy downtown street, beside an idling car parked the wrong way, people passing me and snickering at me, still shaking from a Jerry Lewis shakedown, an eighty-five-dollar ticket on my windshield, waiting for the Auto Club to set me free. Ain't show business grand?

And the best was yet to come!

From that moment on, every time my cell phone rang I had Jerry seizures. But for the rest of Thursday and all of Friday there were no calls from the Lewis brigade. All was calm, all was bright. But, not being the type to leave well enough alone, I called Raemona myself a couple of times; despite my probing, she insisted that everything was running smoothly.

And then the levee broke.

The next time I ran into Jerry Lewis was at the massive Comedy Central bash, a free-for-all in which over a thousand Just For Laughs artists and guests stuff themselves into two Delta Hotel ballrooms. The party starts at midnight, includes an all-night bacon-and-egg breakfast, and is the festival's most popular social event. I had just come from seeing two superb shows we had put on that night—a gala hosted by Alan King that featured two young comedians named Ray Romano and Jon Stewart, and the North American premiere of the now-ubiquitous dance hit *Stomp*. Jerry, meanwhile, had put in his first performance as part of The Just For Laughs 350th Symphony.

Before I describe this harrowing episode, here's another important aside. As I already mentioned, the glorious Lily Tomlin was the host of our Showtime telecast that year. Accompanying Lily to Just For Laughs was a slew of family and friends, including her longtime partner and collaborator, Jane Wagner; her brother, Richard; and a gaggle of her cousins. One such cousin was a guy with poofy curly hair, a twangy southern accent, and a burning desire to meet Jerry Lewis. "Ainduh," he would say to me, "I luhhhve Jerry! I seen all his moovuhs and Lily promised me yuh'd introduce me to him. 'Cause I luhhhhve Jerry!" Every time I'd see this country cousin he'd repeat the same drawled-out rap and make me swear on a stack of Bibles that I'd introduce him to his idol because Lily had promised him that I would. And because he luhhhhved Jerry.

Back to the Comedy Central party. As anniversary parties go, this one was a blast. Showtime had given us a pile of extra cash, allowing us to bring acts like Sinbad, Steven Wright, Rita Rudner, Drew Carey, and Penn and Teller[29] to the table. With a double Absolut on the rocks in my hand, I circulated merrily through the throng, shaking hands and greeting friends I only get to see once a year. Then I glanced over at the ballroom's main entrance and saw Jerry tentatively peering in. As a good host should, I put down my glass and walked over to welcome him. "So, how did your show go tonight?" I asked. He responded by closing his hands around my neck.

Throttling and shaking me, Lewis smiled and said, "You Jew bastard! Trying to pull a fast one on me!"

I tried to think of a snappy comeback, but all I could summon up was, "Huh?"

"I saw TV cameras there tonight! I never gave you the right to tape me!"

He hadn't given us that right, but Stabile had. Yet rather than confront a man intent on strangling me in front of hundreds of onlookers, I immediately downshifted into ultrahumble mode: "Jerry, do you think

---

[29] Teller, the silent half of the postmodern magic duo, tells this great story of his close encounter with the King of Comedy. "In 1992 I was on the phone with my parents, and I told them that Jerry Lewis was next to me. They didn't believe me, so I handed him the phone, and he did a full-blown Jerry: 'Yeah, I'm here with your fucking idiot kid.' They laughed. Later they told me it was the best Jerry Lewis imitation they ever heard."

a little nothing like me would try to put one over on a respected megastar like you? Do you think I'd try to film you without having the rights? I negotiated them with Joe. I have a signed agreement!" Lewis loosened his grip and softened his approach.

"Well, I knew nothing about it," he replied, "but if Joey signed it, I'll live up to it. Let's put it this way: if you can show me this agreement by tomorrow afternoon, signed, I'll apologize, I'll respect you, I'll love you, and I'll give you a great show on Sunday [the Showtime show]. If you don't show me this agreement by tomorrow, I'll still love you, respect you, and perform for you . . ." And then his face turned to stone ". . . but I'll make the rest of your life a living hell, understand?"

As if all of this weren't bad enough, I had another situation to contend with at the same time. Remember Lily's loopy cousin? He'd begun to gravitate towards Jerry the minute he'd spotted him, and while Jerry was busy garroting me, he positioned himself in my line of vision and started making conspicuous hand gestures—pointing to himself and to my assailant, indicating that after this public strangulation had run its course, I would have to live up to my promise and introduce him.

I nodded to Jerry, acknowledging my full comprehension of the situation, pulled the hayseed over, and did the dirty deed. "Uh, Jerry," I said, shaken, both literally and figuratively, "this fellow is Lily's cousin. He's a real big fan, and Lily made me promise to introduce him to you." "Ugh," Jerry grunted as he turned towards Lily's ecstatic family member. "Jerry, I luhhhhhve you!" the cousin enthused, and before his prey could retreat, he engulfed Jerry in a bear hug. It was a scene from a Fellini movie projected backwards. Stunned, Jerry peered over the cousin's shoulder and shouted, to no one in particular, *"Who do I have to fuck to get out of here?"*

I was finally able to break them up, and Jerry bolted, but he ran right into Alan King, who insisted that he stick around for a drink. The two comedy Moseses made their way to the middle of the room, the crowd parting for them like the Red Sea. Meanwhile, I made a beeline for my assistant, Robin Altman, disturbing her schmooze session with handsome New York press attaché Michael O'Brien. "Robin, remember the Jerry Lewis contract? Did we ever get it signed?"

Unsure of what this was all about, she said, "I think so." When I told

Jerry Lewis: the backstage reenactment of our infamous strangulation episode.
I smiled a whole lot less the first time around.

her she had to get back to the office right away and find it, she complained, "But the office is a shambles!" She was right. From June on,
we'd tossed just about everything onto a "to file" pile. I knew I had that
contract somewhere, but under the combined influence of alcohol and
panic, one tends to doubt reality.

"Robs," I said, "you've got to find that document, make twenty pho-
tocopies of it, and call me as soon as you do. I don't care what you do,
I don't care what time you call, but do it!" It was now after 1:30 A.M.,
but off to the office went my assistant, and back to the bar went I. "I
need a triple," I said, trotting instead of pacing.

And then another memorable party moment occurred, this one
costarring Lewis and King.

Seeing the two comedic icons hanging out in such close proximity
was too much for Mike MacDonald to handle. The only comedian to
appear at each and every Just For Laughs since its inception, Mike was

an aficionado of the genre. Unlike many of his peers, he had studied his comic predecessors, and he had the utmost respect for them. To pay homage to the pioneers standing mere inches away from him, Mike made his way over, got on his knees, and bowed, lying facedown at their feet. Lewis glanced down, shrugged, gave King a "let's split this scene" look, stepped on and then over the prone worshipper, and quickly exited the festivities. King followed suit. When Mike looked up, his idols had vanished.

By now it was getting late. It was 3:00 A.M., and still no word from Robin. Another drink. A half-hour later, she rang my hotel room. "Got it!" she shouted. I ran downstairs, jumped into a cab, picked Robin up at the office, and charged over to the Four Seasons. We personally slipped copies under every door of Jerry's suite. As insurance, we sent up two more copies via the hotel concierge, and each of us held on to a bunch in case there was a confrontation the next day. No news is good news, and I didn't hear from Jerry on Saturday. I did, however, call Raemona, who told me that Jerry had received the contract, called Joe in Las Vegas, and confirmed everything. Mission accomplished!

The next time I ran into Jerry was in a dressing room corridor of the St. Denis Theater on Sunday afternoon during the Showtime rehearsal. He quickly reiterated his conversation with Joe for me, and, since the strangulation incident had become the talk of the festival, he replicated it for the backstage photographers, much to the delight of the performers and technicians milling about. All is calm, all is bright.

The Showtime show was superb. Lily resurrected beloved characters like Ernestine the switchboard operator and lounge singer Tommy Velour. Jerry's walk-on received a standing ovation of gargantuan proportions. His Hall of Fame acceptance speech brought many to tears, and he even tacked on a personal thank-you to yours truly before he walked off to another ovation. Immediately following the evening's curtain call, he summoned me to his dressing room. "Oh Christ, what now?" I thought. There he sat, alone and serene. "Close the door," he said.

I prepared myself for the worst. At least when he strangled me I had witnesses. Here, he could kill me unseen and claim self-defense.

"I want to apologize," he said humbly.

"Aw, forget it Jerry. It's all right."

"No, no, no! I accused you of something, and I was wrong. You were a man of your word. You said you had a contract, and you did. You said you'd deliver it to me, and you did. You were right, and I was wrong."

"Apology appreciated and accepted. It's over. Let's call it a day."

"There's just one more thing," he said.

I saw a little box at the corner of his makeup table. I thought maybe he had a small parting gift for me. Well, sort of. But it wasn't in the box. Jerry's "one more thing" was a tirade against the amount of tax that had been taken off his fee. I tried to explain the Canada-U.S. tax treaty, but to no avail. Knowing full well that arguing was futile, I said I would look into a solution.

For three weeks Jerry called my office, the last time from the set of the MDA Telethon. I'll never forget our final words.

"Jerry, there's nothing I can do about it," I pleaded. "Taxes have to be paid. I can't fuck with the government."

"No," he yelled, "but you can't fuck Jerry, either!"

I never knew what he meant by that, but believe me, wherever I go, to this day, I'm always on my guard, looking out for a stray pair of hands.

Postscript: Our paths crossed again, albeit unbeknownst to Jerry, in Aspen, in February 2000. Jerry was being honored by HBO's U.S. Comedy Arts Festival during an afternoon session hosted by Martin Short. I made it my mission to score tickets for myself and my business partner Garner Bornstein, and on my way to the event, like a modern-day Dorothy off to see the wizard, I dragged along Todd Schwartz, an old NBC friend, now with VH–1. "Trust me, it won't be boring," I assured them both as we waited in line. "I guarantee you he'll shoot off his mouth or do something controversial that will cause a ruckus."

For over an hour, led masterfully by Short, Jerry charmed the socks off the crowd. His anecdotes were hilarious, the clips they had chosen were adorable, and even when he pompously crowed about how much money he has made in his lifetime, he somehow did it with charisma. Like Lily's cousin, you just wanted to hug the guy. "Some ruckus," sneered

Todd. "This is about as controversial as a bowl of ice cream," scoffed Garner.

"We have time for one final question," announced Short, and he pointed to a woman in the crowd. "Mr. Lewis, what do you think about female comedians?" she asked. *Boinnng!* Lewis's response conjured up ghosts of 1986. "I don't like any female comedians," he replied. "A woman doing comedy doesn't offend me, but it sets me back a bit. I, as a viewer, have trouble with it. I think of her as a producing machine that brings babies in the world." The electricity in the room started to short-circuit. "But what about Lucille Ball or Carol Burnett?" Short interjected, trying to salvage the reputation of his guest and calm the mood of the mob. "Surely you think they're funny, surely you loved Lucy..."

"Nope," Lewis smiled. Short moaned. "Aw, you had 'em! You had them in the palm of your hand! You owned this room!" he wailed dejectedly. But the cat was out of the bag and scratching up a storm. Short wrapped up, but, once again, the media rushed off to file their disparaging reports, which, once again, appeared throughout North America.

I turned to Todd and Garner, and although the right side of my face was twitching uncontrollably, I beamed with the delight of once again being right.

S E V E N

SEX AND DRUGS
AND ROCKET BUTT

One of the great slogans slapped on the Just For Laughs experience was, "It's summer camp for adults!" Although I have my doubts about the "adult" part of that catchphrase, our annual gathering of stars, star wannabes, and powerful showbiz people who could turn the latter into the former made for an interesting social cocktail. The gender positioning, the sexual politics, the flamboyant flirting, the strange disappearances, the not-so-secret rendezvous, and the resulting gossip were often more entertaining than the shows on our stages. So, with apologies to the late Ian Dury, the details revealed in this chapter should be all your brain and body need.

SEX

Is it hot in here, or is it just the festival's July time frame? My God, if I had a dollar for every illicit affair, every one-night stand during my tenure, Bill Gates would be my butler and the Sheik of Brunei my pool boy. Comedians, particularly the male breed, aren't known to be very discriminating when it comes to the female company they keep,[30] but at Just For Laughs, the order of business was downgraded further still to, "If it

---

[30] A standard industry joke: How do you make a comedian horny? Carry a tray and serve him a drink.

moves, make your move." Every year we had to print up extra access passes by the gross for comedians whose "girlfriends" just so happened to arrive from out of town at the last minute. One *Star Search* talent scout was on constant cruise control; he was notorious for luring potential "spokesmodels" to his hotel room, where, of course, he had application forms just waiting to be filled out.

There were a few funnymen whose randy reputations not only preceded them—they did so by about a month and a half. One such "stickman" (to use Bob Williams's term) was Roland Magdane, a dashing Frenchman I befriended in New York and worked with when he moved to L.A. So smooth, so slick, so charming was this modern-day Casanova that I feared he would never make it out of his hotel room when we booked him for the festival. As a preventive measure, festival accountant Mark Goldman and I added a "no shtupping" clause to his contract in 1988, threatening to withhold payment should he have sex within twenty-four hours before a performance. How we could possibly enforce that stipulation was anyone's guess, but we'd sure have fun trying.

Sex spilled out from behind closed doors and into public view on many a disgraceful occasion. In 1989 a special midnight show by hypnotist Tom De Luca caused quite the commotion in the Delta Hotel's sardine-packed Opus II ballroom. One of De Luca's participants, a nondescript young lady of about twenty, became an instant celebrity because of her high-flying impression of a ballerina . . . and because she was underwearless under her skirt. A decade later, just down the hall, another young lady interrupted a live radio interview with Howie Mandel, asking the star if he would like to see her elephant tattoo. After being hounded for about five minutes, Howie finally acquiesced, at which time the woman hoisted her skirt high and paraded bottomless until she was shooed away by hotel security. The crowd, attracted like moths to her pelvic flame, hissed and hooted heartily, making for great "mind theater" radio.

Another sordid radio story concerns the recurring debauchery caused by Bruce Hills, Willie Mercer (now one of Hollywood's hottest managers), and yours truly on CJAD, one of the festival's official broadcast sponsors. Every late June, evening talk-show host Peter Anthony

Holder would have the three of us on for an open-line prefestival roundup. No reflection on Peter, but we were all exhausted at that time of year, and we needed something other than Peter's witticisms to spice up the proceedings. The first year we brought in a sizeable liquor selection and consumed it on the air.[31] The second year we went a step further; again we drank copiously, but we ordered supper up to the station, as well, and we brought the confused deliveryman into our interview. In the third year we raised the bar to new heights. Once more we drank and ordered supper, but, as a special treat, I also ordered a bikini-clad "escort" to serve it . . . and to passionately massage the shoulders of whichever of us was talking. As planned, Peter played along and asked a wary Bruce most of the questions, which made for some mighty uncomfortable-sounding answers.

As revenge, Bruce brought us to a strip bar just up the street from the radio station. Strippers were a common sight at Just For Laughs shows; payback, I guess, as Just For Laughs guests were an even more common sight at strip shows. One Montreal club, Chez Paree, was so popular with festival artists and VIPs that we actually listed its Stanley Street address as an official venue. More than just a place to leer, Chez Paree became the festival's deal-making hub; there were nights when just about everyone there, including the strippers, was wearing flashy, laminated Just For Laughs access passes.[32]

A little after midnight, as we celebrated another wild night on Peter's show with loud music and more drinks, my cell phone rang. It was Jodi Lieberman, the sweet, innocent intern who had been promoted to head of festival logistics in 1997 (and who became the event's key programmer in 2000). Known as "The Troop" for being the ultimate "do it until it's done" trooper, she was still at the office putting out

---

[31] We were laughing so hard that one caller remarked, "You guys sound like you're having a lot of fun." "Of course we are," slurred Willie. "We're drunk!" Bruce was horrified; there was no way he was going to be accused of being inebriated in public. "Speak for yourself, Jim," he said haughtily. It took me a second to realize what was wrong, but then I demanded, "Hey, who the hell is Jim?" Bruce was so gone that he'd forgotten Willie's name. We fell off our chairs in hysterics.

[32] Gilbert Gottfried was so enamored with the place that it became his second home—literally. One summer the airport car dropped him off at the club before he'd even checked into his hotel, and our transport department was instructed to pick him up there before, and deliver him back there after, each of his performances.

fires. Oh, if she only knew where she was reaching her esteemed bosses!

I ran to the back of the club to hear her better. Yup, yet another calamity. The plane carrying George Daugherty, the creator and conductor of the Bugs Bunny on Broadway outdoor megashow we were presenting, was once more delayed flying out of Chicago. I had planned to greet him at the Delta Hotel at about 11:00 P.M., then at 1:00 A.M., but now, I learned, he wouldn't be on the ground until 3:00 at the earliest. Oh, well, at least I had a place to hang out until then. I returned to our table, in front of which the evening's main act—a friendly couple of gals; real friendly, in fact—were doing some sort of nude synchronized tumbling routine.

"What's wrong?" Willie asked.

"Another delay," I answered. "The guy from Bugs Bunny on Broadway . . ."

"Bugs Bunny on Broadway?" came the ecstatic reply—but, oddly enough, from the stage. One of the girls, the one on her back on the floor, popped her head out from beneath her buff buddy's butt.

"Did I hear you say, Bugs Bunny on Broadway?" she reiterated.

Another surreal experience. I was engaged in conversation with a prone stripper about our most family-oriented spectacle that year.

"You have good ears," I complimented her.

"I really want to see that show!" she raved.

"Speak to him," I said, pointing to Willie, the only single man among us. "I'm sure he'll get you free tickets."

DRUGS

Quality over quantity. There's only one Just For Laughs drug saga that I feel comfortable recounting—but, oh, what a saga it is!

The story you are about to read is true. To protect the innocent—or perhaps the guilty; that's still up in the air—I won't reveal the names of those involved (I won't even reveal the year, as some of you more astute readers with access to our old press releases may have the urge to play detective). But every other detail is accurate. Strike up the *Dragnet* theme.

It was Thursday. Friday, actually. Friday morning, real early. Another long Just For Laughs night. Another party pierced, another celebration shattered, by the ring of my cell phone. On the other end was Willie Mercer, huffing and puffing. "We have a problem," he groaned. Yeah, get in line. At this time of year, I subsist on a strict diet of problems. I eat 'em up and spit 'em out. This one was a drug bust. I'd been down that path already. A year or so before, another festival guest, an L.A. disc jockey, was walking through an alley with a joint between his lips. Paid a fine and went back home to spin.

But this was a tougher one to digest. Willie shed light on the circumstances. Two of our VIP guests had been busted for a biggie: possession with the intent to traffic. It seems that a FedEx package, filled with the wackiest of weeds, was sent to their Delta hotel room. As one of the recipients tore open the envelope, a team of cops tore open his door. His yarn was that he had no idea who had sent it; FedEx envelopes flow like water during Just For Laughs. Not a good enough excuse. Off to the hoosegow went a sharp-tongued comic and his manager, a Hollywood bigwig with the Midas touch.

And that was just the bad news.

Worse news? The fact that the comic was slated to host a live TV show late the next night. We had less than twenty-four hours to spring him. And we had to do so without arousing suspicion. Luckily, I was in the right place at the right time. To my right was a powerful friend of the festival. He took my phone and roused a well-connected lawyer friend of his from his slumbers.

An hour later, we were meeting. Two hours later, the lawyer was at the police station. The charge was serious. The boys wouldn't be bounced that night. So we made a plan. The lawyer would hit the courthouse in the morning, seeking bail. Meanwhile, we'd cover for the guys at the festival, saying that they had gone north of the city to the Laurentian Mountains for some rest and relaxation before the big show. Nobody was to know the truth. Not our partners, not the comics—and especially not the broadcast network.

Time for a bit of shut-eye. It was 6:00 A.M., and the sun was already up, a beacon for the big day ahead. From 10:00 A.M. to 2:00 P.M., nothing.

Rehearsal was at 6:00 P.M. It was almost 3:00 P.M. when I finally heard from the lawyer. He had good news. He could spring the boys. All we had to do was put up their bail. Forty thousand dollars. By 5:00 P.M., or else. After that, it would be the weekend, and the boys would be spending a long one inside the slammer if we didn't come through. I called our bank from my hotel room. There was not enough time for them to prepare a certified check that big and for me to get it over to the courthouse. I needed someone with deep pockets. Fortuitously, that person was an elevator ride away: the manager of the Delta Hotel. I gave him hundreds of thousands in business every summer; the least he could do was front me forty Gs. In cash.

The manager came through without much arm-twisting. Made me sign a promissory note, opened the safe in front of a witness, and stuffed a briefcase with bills. Then I had to deliver it. Obviously, I didn't call FedEx or a bike courier. Couldn't do it myself, either; I had work to do at the hotel, work that put me in the media spotlight. I was expected to make appearances. So, I called the lawyer. We didn't have much time, and he couldn't show his well-known face around the hotel lobby. The compromise: he would send over an associate. "Wait," I said. "How will I recognize him? I'm not handing forty grand over to just anybody." The lawyer laid it out for me. I would sit on a couch in the lobby, the briefcase on the floor between my feet. The associate would appear, carrying a brown alligator briefcase filled with official documents. He'd sit down next to me and place his briefcase next to mine. He'd nod twice; I'd nod once. Then we'd make the switch. Real cloak-and-dagger stuff. Finally, the associate would take the cash away, leaving me with the legal papers.

Sure enough, it all went off like clockwork. Nobody suspected that anything was going down. At 5:00, the lawyer called. The deal was done. By 5:30 the two jailbirds were flying into the hotel through the back door. After they'd showered, they were taken over to the venue. The show went off without a hitch. Actually, the fatigue and stress seemed to enrich the comic's performance. There was more bitter in his bittersweet.

Of course, the court case would be coming up later, but now, relieved and free, the comic and his manager were able to laugh again. They told tales of the joint. Hilarious tales. Like how the manager promised to bring some of his other clients to town for a concert to benefit the Policeman's Brotherhood—provided that they let him out right away. Like how the manager explained to a $35,000-a-year cop what kind of insane money a manager makes in Tinseltown.

"One thing," the curious manager asked me. "What does 'tayul' mean?"

"Tayul?" I responded. "Oh, 'ta yeulle.' That's an abbreviation for the French expression, 'ferme ta gueule.'"

"Which means?"

"Literally, 'close your mouth.' But it's usually expressed as, 'shut the hell up.' Why do you ask?"

Ill at ease with the explanation, the manager said, "Uh, that's what the cops kept saying to me."

"Good advice," I said.

"Taken."

ROCKET BUTT

It was only seen once at Just For Laughs, on Thursday, July 19, 1990, but Chris Lynam's blazing-butt routine has taken on a magical, mythical status. Although witnessed by only 430 or so people at Club Soda, like most feats of this ilk—Don Larsen's perfect game, Mark McGwire's sixty-second home run—tens of thousands will someday claim to have been there and seen it live.

Lynam himself called the finale to his act "Banger up the Bum." It involved a massive Roman candle, which he inserted . . . You know what? Better you should hear it from an actual eyewitness. Here's how Stephen Saban described the scene in the October 1990 edition of *Details* magazine:

> Suddenly, Malcolm Hardee reappeared on stage *completely naked*, his scrotum magnificent in the footlights. He sat on a chair behind Lynam, crossed his legs, lit a cigarette, and waited. Lynam turned around to prepare for the pyrotechnic portion of his act, spotted Hardee, and appeared surprised. He went to the back of the stage, bent over, his short skirt revealing his ass, then began to strip. Hardee casually approached the mike.

"You've probably noticed by now," he said without inflection, "that I have extremely large testicles." The audience lost it. Hardee said he would light the firecracker in Lynam's bum. Then it all happened so quickly. Lynam, naked too, bent over, his privates tucked between his legs. Hardee touched a match to Lynam's ass. Flames and sparks shot out an incredible distance as Lynam spun around the room filled with the strains of "There's No Business like Show Business." Then the stage was empty. True story. I don't make this stuff up.

In that one defining moment Chris Lynam became the talk of the 1990 festival—and every one that followed. Not a year has gone by that Lynam's death-defying derriere isn't mentioned by the media in preview stories or by the assembled artist/industry mix. Unforgettable? To his credit, and as testimony to his marketing brilliance, Lynam has never repeated this fiery finale, but it plays on and on and on in people's minds and in their stories. As Saban put it, "Lynam's asshole was on everyone's lips."

Who was this scene-stealer, this purveyor of one of Just For Laughs' most indelible images? Chris Lynam was an anarchistic street performer known as Chris the Piss, as dangerous to himself as to his audience, when I first met him in London. Weathered, emaciated, hair sprayed in a straight-up eruption, he looked like a cross between Keith Richards and Eraserhead. I learned a bit more about Chris when we met at a West End members only club he belonged to (one had to slither down a long, skinny alley to enter). He was born in Zimbabwe, and, most astonishingly, he was a married father of three. While Bruce Hills and I loved him, we worried that he might not be able to adjust to the relatively mainstream confinements of our event. But, when we heard that London Weekend Television producer Juliet Blake had given him a TV shot and that he'd actually "behaved" while doing it, we made our move.

That move did not sit well with our British broadcasting partners, Tiger Television. Particularly suspicious was executive producer Charles Brand (who has gone on to produce award-winning films like *Billy Elliott*). "He's your responsibility," Charles warned us, flashing his strange, up-

Chris Lynam's infamous Rocket Butt routine.
A tough act to follow, to say the least.

side-down frown. "He's not coming to the festival as part of the official British contingent." "Fine," I responded. "He's part of my contingent."

Maybe I spoke too soon. The Chris Lynam who finally touched down on North American soil was a one-man, three-ring circus of problems. Making the most of Air Canada's open-bar policy, he arrived drunk. His luggage—although sober—did not arrive at all. And, the last straw, his hotel room wasn't ready.

I went off to the hotel myself to deal with Chris and douse some of the flames. Instead, I ended up dealing with Jack Nicholson as The Joker. Lynam was a madman, but a smiling one. We rectified the room situation right away, but not before Lynam had come to within milli-seconds of igniting a major brawl. At the check-in desk was adorable Christy LaBove, wife of comic Carl LaBove, who was at Just For Laughs with the dangerous Sam Kinison. I introduced Chris to Christy. What was I thinking?

"Oooooh, Christy," Lynam purred as he stroked her arm. Carl came shooting over like a scud missile. I managed to hold him back, saying, "Please Carl, he's drunk. He's had a rough day." Carl vowed, "It'll get a lot rougher if he ever looks at my wife again!" I had averted a major scene, but the imbroglio was, of course, witnessed by none other than Charles Brand, who was passing by to pick up a FedEx delivery. "Your contingent, your responsibility," he said. "I told you so!"

One last river to cross: Lynam's missing luggage. His first show was that night, and he didn't have the little girl's red skating outfit he used for one of his more poignant numbers. After sobering up and cooling down, he met a girl as petite as he, and he shared his predicament with her. She was Dom Irrera's girlfriend, and, luckily for Chris, she was as cordial and selfless as her boyfriend. When Dom returned to his room that night, he found his generous girlfriend going through her wardrobe with Lynam, who was trying on different outfits. Dom gazed at Lynam in disbelief and then turned to his girlfriend. "See how good that dress can look if you lose a couple pounds?" he deadpanned.

One of the more interesting ripple effects of Lynam's firestorm was the ascent of Tim Allen. As I mentioned earlier in this tome, in 1990 Tim was the new and rising comic who had been given the task of leading off our Showtime gala. Honing his act for the special, Tim wedged in every warm-up set he could at various Montreal clubs. One such set was at Club Soda on that fateful Thursday, July 19.

It would not rank among his easiest performances, for Tim had drawn the unenviable task of following the Chris Lynam/Malcolm Hardee experience. Tim made a valiant attempt, but he quickly realized the pointlessness of it all. Instead of wilting or wimping out, however, Tim turned the tables; he changed directions and did six minutes on how impossible it is to follow Chris Lynam, concluding each bit with the words "up my ass." The crowd ate it up with a spoon. They appreciated the fact that he'd chosen to go with the flow, and they rewarded him with a standing ovation.

By the next night, Tim Allen had become a media and industry golden boy, and he smoked the St. Denis Theater audience. You know the rest of the story by now. Well, most of it. Tim did so well that his performance was nominated for a 1990 ACE, an award that recognized

SEX AND DRUGS AND ROCKET BUTT

excellence in cable programming. He was up against some heavy-weights, including Billy Crystal and his Midnight Train to Moscow magnum opus, and he didn't have a chance. Imagine the supreme shock he felt when he heard his name announced as the winner.[33]

Unlike other Hollywood denizens, who ignore their roots and forget their humble beginnings, and despite being dazed and having no pre-pared acceptance speech, Tim knew whom to thank. His wife, who had stuck with him through the hard times. His managers, who believed when no one else did. The Showtime braintrust, who kept the faith. And he saved the best for last. "And especially to Rocket Butt, the guy I had to follow in Montreal," Tim said to the puzzled, black-tie industry crowd. "This one's for you!"

---

[33] Even more surprised was HBO president Michael Fuchs. At the awards ceremony he leapt from his seat and cried, "Who the hell is Tim Allen?" A few months later he learned.

EVERYTHING'S COMING UP ROSEANNE

It was 1986 when I took my first sip of the steaming personality stew named Roseanne. Granted, she's an acquired taste, but even back then Roseanne stood out—far, far out—from the standard array of female comedians who moaned about how small their boobs were or what boobs their boyfriends were. It was a Thursday night when I first saw her perform live. She came roaring into L.A.'s Improv like a runaway train, parting the crush of tourists and industry hangers-on clustered at the club's entry. At that point she was relatively new to Hollywood, but a killer appearance with Johnny Carson on *The Tonight Show* had made her a larger-than-life persona among the legion of comedic clones in the clubs. She didn't wait for scheduled club spots; she just showed up and went on. I was enamored with her Domestic Goddess routine and tried to book her as soon as she left the stage.

I must've been good. Five years later she showed up.

By that time she was the hottest star on TV and one of the most controversial figures in showbiz. It had been a year since her infamous crotch-grab-and-spit national anthem incident, and she was embarking on her first-ever national tour of "soft-seaters" (industry parlance for theaters as opposed to "hard-seat" venues, like bars and clubs). The timing couldn't have been better. We managed to score one of the last open dates on her tour, and we extended the already nerve-fraying 1991 festival (Sadowitz, the parade, Milton Berle . . . need I go on?) another day to accommodate her.

We signed the contract for Roseanne Barr on May 10. Her thirty-three-page rider was standard, perhaps even a tad spartan for a star of her magnitude: no booze, lots of water, fruit juice, and vegetables. The only clause that raised the most infinitesimal of red flags involved security. Her people were requesting a little bit more than we were used to providing (including "one security person at all times from the moment when she arrives at the venue until her limousine leaves the venue"), but nothing excessive ("Ms. Barr prefers that security personnel not be dressed in police-type uniforms"). So, over and above the usual festival team, we hired an outside firm of "shtarkers" (that's Yiddish for over-sized gentlemen with violent tendencies). Small price to pay to keep a big star happy.

About a month later Roseanne Barr became Roseanne Arnold, marrying Tom Arnold, a cast member of her TV show and the obvious choice as her opening act on the tour. Whoops! Unexpected name change! Call back the programs, the ad mattes, and the posters! Our communications team bitched and moaned over the extra work and expense. "Relax," I told them. " This should be our biggest problem with the show." Guess what? It wasn't.

But first, the good news. Roseanne's Just For Laughs closing concert was the first on the tour to sell out. We considered adding a second show, but extending the event into Tuesday would've provoked a full-fledged staff mutiny. We decided to do just one show, but we'd do it perfectly.

Perhaps the person most obsessed with delivering this perfection was the person who'd been most ecstatic about Roseanne's festival appearance in the first place: my assistant, Robin Altman. Any description I would attempt to make of Robin in these pages would cause her to compulsively analyze each word—each syllable!—for deeper meaning, so let's just say that I love her a lot and appreciate every moment we spent together over the better part of a decade (including those in which she threw sunglasses and ashtrays at me, and I threw staplers and computer discs at her).

Upon hearing the first hint of a rumor that we were working on

Roseanne, Robin sprang into action. She had read Roseanne's autobiography, *My Life as a Woman*, and, as another hardworking underdog of the female species fighting to survive in the boy's club of show business (I learned that speech by heart!), she related to the book, its message, and especially its author. "Please!" Robin begged. "You have to let me do more on this show! I must meet Roseanne! She's my idol! I have so much to tell her! I want to tell her how much her words mean to me!"

So, I put Robin in charge of Roseanne's comfort (killing two birds with one stone, I figured—I was keeping both assistant and star happy). Robin would provide an additional layer of service, ensuring that the hotel, limo, and dressing room facilities of our illustrious guest would go far beyond the norm. This would also guarantee that Robin got a face-to-face with her heroine. Robin took to her assignment like a military commander. Only the finest, freshest mineral water would touch Roseanne's lips. Her limo would be stocked with tapes of the girl groups that Robin knew Roseanne loved. And, as the pièce de résistance, Robin would put together an offering of festival merchandise for Roseanne unlike any other ever assembled.

Her attention to detail in this regard was staggering. I remember her tearing into the St. Denis Theater hours before Roseanne's show, plastic bags full of Just For Laughs loot exploding from her hands. T-shirts, sweatshirts, stuffed animals, coffee mugs—everything we produced, and in mass quantities. Then, like a sculptress, Robin arranged the booty on the long dressing room table with engineered precision. Shirts were color-coordinated so as not to clash with each other. Toys were stuffed into mugs for a dainty floral-arrangement effect. Ever the perfectionist, Robin bent to table level, closed one eye, and squinted the other to ensure equidistance and the symmetry of her layout (I could swear she had a protractor to measure angles). Perhaps it was just my extreme fatigue, but I almost shed a tear upon viewing the final result. My little assistant had become the Michaelangelo of memorabilia. She had created a modern-day Sistine Chapel of poly-cotton blend, plush velour, and ceramic on a dressing room tabletop.

The St. Denis Theater is a madhouse on gala show days, but that Monday afternoon we spent a few quiet, lazy hours waiting for Roseanne. The stage had been stripped of its splendor, and all that remained was a plain black curtain. With only a stool and microphone as technical requirements, there was no need for rehearsal or sound check. It was truly the calm before the storm.

At about 6:00 P.M., two hours before the show, the additional security forces arrived. Three big guys were stationed backstage; one at each entry door and one onstage. Two more were in the theater itself, positioned at each side of the proscenium. And then there was Roseanne's "shadow," waiting for his cue to follow the star.

A little over an hour later we got the call from the limo. Roseanne and Tom were on their way. It was T-minus-ten-minutes. Everyone was in place backstage. Robin was at the stage door, ready to act as our official greeter, almost shivering with excitement.

And we waited. And waited . . . and waited . . .

And . . . where the hell was she? It was 7:35. We'd gotten the call a half-hour ago! Even in the worst traffic, it doesn't take this long to get to the theater from the hotel! Someone called the limo driver, and then we really got scared. He swore that he had dropped Roseanne and Tom off at the artists' entrance a while ago. But this couldn't be! Robin was waiting at the artists' entrance, and she was still waiting. Jesus Christ! Roseanne had vanished!

Just then, I felt the strangest sensation, as if my back was being pierced by two slow drills. I turned around and looked down the backstage hall, all the way to the other end. There she was. Glowering. Definitely unhappy. Shoulders hunched and lowered as if ready to charge at me like a rhino. If looks could kill, I'd be cremated, my ashes mixed with water and thrown into a trough for a pack of starving wild boar. Andy, meet Roseanne!

Tom Arnold was following behind his wife, but he intercepted me before I could speak to her. "Don't say anything," he warned. "Just get her into the dressing room." Although it seemed like an eternity, it was only a few minutes before Tom emerged from the dressing room with the official story. He was royally pissed off, but he remained gracious and calm. It seemed that, yes, the limo driver had dropped them off at the artists' entrance—but at the wrong theater. You see, the St. Denis is a two-room complex, and the driver had left Roseanne and Tom at the St. Denis II; it being a Monday night, the place was dark and empty.

After winding through a maze of dank underground corridors, the stars of our show finally found their way to the right theater, but they'd been forced to enter through the back passageway. The security guard stationed there spoke only French, and he didn't know the difference between Roseanne and a mushroom pizza. All he knew were his orders: the star is coming in the other side, and nobody enters through this door without a pass. Roseanne, frustrated, passless, and haggard from the hike, finally made him see it her way. I shudder to think how. "Well, look on the bright side," I told Tom cheerily. "At least the security system is working." He was unamused.

We didn't see Roseanne again until intermission. Although she'd hung out in the wings during Tom's opening set, we were all too scared to go anywhere near her. But we had to break the ice during halftime. To help promote the show, the Montreal *Gazette* and Just For Laughs had put together a contest, and the grand prize was a backstage meet-and-greet with Roseanne. Since Roseanne wanted to leave the venue as soon as possible after the show was over, she'd asked to meet the winner during intermission. I timidly knocked on her dressing room door and introduced the winner: a suburban housewife who had brought along another suburban housewife for good measure.

When the perfunctory greetings and Kodak moments were over, the two women were ushered out. But before they disappeared through the door, one of them called out, "Wait! Roseanne, it was such a thrill meeting you. Can we at least have a souvenir to remember this by?" Roseanne's eyes slowly surveyed the dressing room. They came to a stop at Robin's shrine. Walking over to the table, she tore through the intricate assemblage of items and piled them unceremoniously in the women's arms. "Here—take this crap!" The tabletop was swept bare.

Robin, who witnessed all of this, took the hit like a pro, never letting her proud smile dissipate—although I noticed the corner of her lips quiver ever so slightly. I guess all great artists must suffer somewhat. At least Robin would have her redemption, her private audience, when the show was over.

Alas, it never came to pass. Roseanne delivered what she was con-tracted to deliver—an hour and ten minutes of rip-roarin', in-your-face comedy. As soon as it was over, mere seconds after her final "Goodnight!," with Tom running interference, she sped up the backstage stairs. She would take no more chances with overeffective security. Waiting for her was the open-doored limo, its engine humming with environmentally irresponsible yet artist-friendly efficiency. Before Robin could even offer her book to be autographed, Roseanne was on her way to the airport, leaving a decimated audience and my disillusioned assistant in her wake.

But worry not. Robin would get her chance six years later. By that time she had been promoted to director of communications for the festival. One fine day she strolled into my office to tell me about a brainstorm she'd just had. Roseanne's sitcom had just ended its decade-long run on ABC, so why not stage a full-blown tribute to the star? As luck would have it, about three weeks prior to this I had run into David Tochterman, then a high-ranking exec at Carsey-Werner Productions, at the bar in the L.A. Four Seasons Hotel. Carsey-Werner was the studio powerhouse that produced *Roseanne* (as well as Brett Butler's *Grace under Fire* and Cybill Shepherd's short-lived sitcom), and Tochterman agreed to be our liaison within the company and help put this thing together. Sure enough, he got the green light from within and set me up with the legendary Jeff Wald, a former rock-music kingpin and onetime husband of singer Helen Reddy. Wald was now managing Roseanne.[34]

Along with Jon Peters and Peter Guber, Wald was the living embodiment (amazingly still living) of the drug-fueled Hollywood eighties.[35] Over the years his stable had included everyone from Donna Summer, to Crosby, Stills & Nash, to Chicago. A survivor among countless burn-outs, Wald had seen it all and done it all twice over. He had also just orchestrated a multizillion-dollar talk-show contract for Roseanne with Kingworld and booked her as the wicked witch in the king-size version of *The Wizard of Oz* at Madison Square Garden. Wald did nothing on a small scale, so we had to create something mammoth to impress him.

As tributes go, our Roseanne tribute, set for Saturday, July 26, was a monster. Code named Just For Laughs Kisses Roseanne's Ass, it was to

---

[34] By this point Roseanne had dropped all family designations and was known, Cher-like, by her first name alone.

[35] Read all about it in the juicy *Hit and Run* by Nancy Griffin and Kim Masters.

be hosted by the acerbic Martin Mull as a special event in a twelve-hundred-seat theater. Emerging from behind a row of fifteen-foot-high letters spelling out her name, Roseanne would be seated on a majestic throne. There she would remain as she was serenaded, lauded, feted, and roasted by a parade of stars, live and on video. We had lined up some whoppers: George Foreman, Fran (*The Nanny*) Drescher, Drew Carey, Moon Zappa, Sandra Bernhard, the *Hollywood Reporter*'s George Christy, producer George Schlatter, James Brolin, Lea Thompson, Cybill Shepherd, Dom Irrera, and Wald himself (surprisingly, none of Roseanne's core group of sitcom costars agreed to participate in any way). To round out the afternoon, the queen would step away from her throne and answer questions from the multitudes gathered before her.

With Roseanne between two TV shows, our timing was perfect. Wald ate it up, and so did the media. Both *Entertainment Weekly* and *Entertainment Tonight* called for passes as soon as the tribute was announced. Trade publication the *Hollywood Reporter* made the event the backbone of its annual Just For Laughs edition, selling costly full-page congratulatory ads to ABC, NBC, CBS, HBO, Kingworld, Madison Square Garden, and another eighties music-management icon named Irving Azoff (whose ad razzed, "Congratulations Roseanne and Jeff Wald. You deserve each other!"). But also lurking within that same edition of the *Reporter* was the catalyst for the near-cancelation of the whole shebang.

Traveling in on the private Kingworld jet, Roseanne was scheduled to land in Montreal on the Thursday before the tribute. In preparation, we had assembled a greeting and operations team that was paramilitary in its responsibilities and personnel. To complement Roseanne's own entourage, we had a twenty-four-hour on-call driver, two off-duty cops to provide security (quite proficient in English, I must add), and a freshly scrubbed teenager to serve as a personal runner. On Tuesday my new assistant, Diane Shatz, had put the whole crew through a dry run. I was walking through the Delta Hotel when she called to give me the all-systems-go, much to my relief. About an hour later my cell phone rang again. This time it was Jeff Wald. We were speaking about ten times a day at this point, and I couldn't wait to give him the latest update. "Hey, Jeff!" I buzzed enthusiastically. "Just spoke to Diane and the team is ready and we can't wait and everyone's so excited . . ." At first he didn't say a word, but I could feel the strain. After what seemed an eternity, he said, "She ain't coming. I've got an unhappy client and we have a big problem."

I was astonished. Every move we'd made had been checked and double-checked with Wald and his people. We had acquiesced to their every demand. Where did we screw up?

"Did you see the *Reporter* today?" Wald asked.

"Yeah," I replied, puzzled. "There were all those ads and . . ."

"Screw the ads," Wald replied. "Did you read the story?"

I hadn't, but I rushed over to our press desk to get a copy. Usually, the story that accompanies the homage section of the *Hollywood Reporter* is no more than publicists' prattle augmented by a couple of laudatory quotes; a puff piece inflated with helium. Now, while the article in question was far from a *National Enquirer* exposé, its inappropriateness—especially among all those brown-nosing ads—scrambled my cerebellum.

Imagine reading this in a tribute written to you: "Roseanne Barr grew up in a poor, dysfunctional Jewish family. Ancestors had died in German concentration camps, and Roseanne's mother—fearing the Nazis were coming to get her family—would sometimes hide in the basement with her four children when the doorbell rang."

Wait, it gets worse. "After she was struck by a car at sixteen (impaling her head on its hood ornament), Roseanne spent a year in a mental hospital. Bouts of starving, gorging and mutilating herself followed." Wait, it gets even worse. "Roseanne moved to Denver and spent the next few years scraping by as a cook, dishwasher, maid, window dresser and prostitute."

Many times, over the years, Roseanne had dug her own grave. This time, writer Alan Waldman was digging mine. Christ, hadn't anybody ever taught this nimrod the difference between a puff piece and a hatchet job? "She's not getting on the plane," Wald announced. "She won't even answer my calls."

In years previous I would've freaked, panicked, and thrown fits. What amazes me to this day was how calm and assured I was, even while the incensed Wald broke the bad news. No pacing. I guess that since I'd survived the John Candy incident in '88, as well as the cancelations of Martin Mull, Richard Lewis, and Paul Reiser in '89, and Michael Richards in '95, I knew I'd get through this one, too. Strangely, I never doubted for a minute that Roseanne would eventually show up. I just knew we'd have to go through hell until she got here.

I couldn't even bring myself to tell Robin, who would've probably committed slow, painful, public suicide as she saw all her hard work vaporize into nothingness. Instead, I hunted down the *Hollywood Reporter*'s Dawn Allen and went ballistic. To add injury to insult, her magazine was *sponsoring* the Roseanne tribute. Through a series of Henry Kissinger–like negotiations that ran into early Wednesday morning, we managed to secure profuse apologies from the *Reporter*'s publisher, Robert Dowling. This, coupled with his assurances that the magazine would cover Roseanne's every word (and promote her upcoming projects) throughout her stay in Montreal, helped Wald to defuse his client's rage and convince her to board the plane.

And then another crisis hit, albeit a minor one compared to Tuesday's shitstorm. About thirty minutes before landing, Wald called me from the plane. "Please don't tell me you're turning around," I groaned. Ben Thomas, Roseanne's former bodyguard and current husband, had an abscessed molar and was in mortal pain. For some reason, Robin had already arranged for my dentist, Dr. Irwin Margolese, to be on twenty-four-hour call, so we rushed Ben over to his office as soon as the plane touched down. A little problem solved, but it went a long way towards showing that we had everything under control this time around.

In appreciation, Wald, Thomas, and Roseanne invited Robin and me to dinner with them that evening. I booked a table at the celebrity hangout Globe (favorite haunt of Robert De Niro, Nicolas Cage, and John Travolta when in town), but, truth be told, I wasn't exactly looking forward to the experience. My previous encounter with Roseanne had been less than stellar, and I was petrified that I'd slip up, say something that would ignite her short fuse, and bring on another turd tornado.

In the few hours that remained before the dinner, I surfed the

Internet, absorbing everything I could about this enigmatic bundle of joy in order to determine her likes and dislikes.[36] What saved the day was a little blurb from *People* magazine mentioning Roseanne's interest in Kaballah, a form of Jewish mysticism. That night, after we'd shared a few pleasantries and ordered our meal, I held my breath and then cautiously remarked to Roseanne, "So I hear that you're into Kaballah . . ." Her cranium tilted like one of those bobbing-head doggies on a car's rear window ledge. Uh-oh. What had I done?

Suddenly, looking like a little girl, she broke into a huge smile. A direct hit! I spent the rest of the night listening to her wax enthusiastically on the subject. Despite Roseanne's somewhat unique vocal stylings, her yapping was music to my ears. When we ran into each other the next day, she actually apologized, saying earnestly, "I hope I didn't bore you talking about Kaballah so much."

Everything went smoothly until tribute day. Attracted by the quality of Montreal's stores and the currency exchange rate, Roseanne spent most of Saturday shopping, and she arrived at the theater a little late. No big deal. But the delay had riled up an already rowdy crowd, and I quickly dropped a few notches on Roseanne's popularity scale as I hurried her onto the stage.

She was met with a huge ovation, and the show worked like a charm. Mull's vicious song was hysterical (his opening line: "We're here today to pay tribute to several of the most talented personalities in showbiz—Roseanne"), Zappa's attempt at stand-up was bawdy (a genitalia routine that predated *The Vagina Monologues* by three years), and Wald almost stole the show by wheeling out a bandaged mannequin on a stretcher and introducing it as Tom Arnold. Throughout it all, Roseanne sat regally, looking divine, laughing along from her divan. But then the incendiary event occurred.

Dom Irrera, who had shared many a stage and road gig with Roseanne in the past, was about to share a particularly nasty story

---

[36] This is not as paranoid as it sounds. When Brett Butler was with us in 1994, one of the no-nos was serving, or even mentioning, melons. I remember alerting our staff to this peculiarity. At first they thought I was kidding. After I'd convinced them I was serious, they *wished* I had been kidding.

Calm before the storm: Martin Mull serenades Roseanne
at her soon-to-be-turbulent tribute.

about the guest of honor.[37] Seeing what was coming and already mor-
tified, Roseanne begged him not to tell the story in front of her new
husband. When Dom made a somewhat joking attempt to continue,
Roseanne threatened to get up and pulverize him. It was a tense
moment (could Alan Waldman be Dom's nom de plume?), eased only
when Dom gave in and left the stage to tumultuous applause.

Watching from the wings, I couldn't help but think of the lines
from the Boomtown Rats song "I Don't Like Mondays" that went: "And
the silicon chip inside her head / Gets switched to overload." Provoked
by Dom, a wilder Roseanne burst from her cage of respectability. First
she sparred with the videos. (To Fran Drescher: "God, she's whiny. I can't

---

[37]My good friend Dom had a propensity for pushing the envelope with unsuitable
anecdotes. At an Israel Bonds dinner in my honor the year before he'd told a hysterical
story that was, unfortunately, so profane that the rabbi banished his wife from the
room before fleeing in horror himself not long afterwards.

take that voice!" To Cybill Shepherd, who sang "We Love You Rosie": "Don't sing . . . please don't sing, Cybill." To Sandra Bernhard: "Hey, isn't that Mick Jagger? No it's the guy from Aerosmith!") Then she sparred with the audience during the question-and-answer session. (To a man who asked who her biggest influence was: "Charles Manson." To a woman who asked if the baby on her show was her own child: "Of course not, you idiot!") She even sparred with me. When I brought out a bouquet of roses to signify the show's end, she cracked: "Oh great, here come the fucking flowers!" After begrudgingly accepting them, she laid the bundle on the podium, took two steps back, and charged at me with outstretched hands, plowing me in the chest. "Now get the fuck off the stage!"

As the show degenerated into a near riot, with screams coming from both the audience and the stage, I stumbled into the wings, chuckling as if Roseanne and I had rehearsed the whole thing. Oh, that gal is such a kidder! I fooled just about everybody—except for Robin. She turned away and held her hands over her mouth to keep herself from bursting into embarrassed laughter. When it was all over, it was as if nothing out of the ordinary had ever happened. Roseanne retired to the *Hollywood Reporter* party that was being thrown in her honor across the street from the theater, and there she schmoozed with industry and media types before heading off to ultrachic seafood eatery Milos for dinner.

By the time Roseanne left Montreal, however, the tribute was the talk of Hollywood—and a lot of other places, too. We had taped the show strictly for festival archive purposes, and suddenly we were getting calls from tabloid TV shows all over the world; everyone was dying for a peek at the bedlam (the tape still lies, unseen, somewhere in Robin's private files). Other networks begged for the broadcast rights, which we didn't have. Scandal sheets from the U.S., England, and Australia printed somewhat exaggerated versions of the Dom-Roseanne dustup and the ensuing brouhaha.

On Tuesday, exactly one week after Wald's first bomb-dropping call, he phoned me again. "I've got a complaint," he growled. "Jeff, I did my best," I protested, "but you were there! You saw what happened! The media basically got it right!" Then Wald explained, "That's not what I'm calling about. My complaint is that I have no complaints. Roseanne and I are the biggest pains in the asses in Hollywood, and we like complaining. We were treated so well, everything went so perfectly, we have nothing to complain about. And that's what's pissing me off."

This time I couldn't wait to break the news to Robin. In spite of her profound fatigue and shell shock, she managed a weary smile. "I think I ought to find another heroine," she said. "Yeah," I replied, "but this time, for the sake of our longevity, make sure she's deceased."

ON THE ROAD AGAIN

A simple equation: an international festival needs international content; international content necessitates international travel. Thus, from day one at Just For Laughs, my globetrotting was nonstop. Incessant airport hopping may have been a big deal back in the fifties, but, let's face it, most businesses these days require their minions to do a fair amount of out-of-town voyaging. In the course of my voyaging, I found myself in some dodgy situations. I lived through earthquakes in L.A., IRA bombings in London, general strikes in France, and a thunderstorm in New York that left me stranded between Kennedy and LaGuardia for two days. But acts of God and acts of terrorism are walks in the park compared to the true occupational hazard of the frequent flyer: other travelers.

There is something about running a comedy event that has a silent-dog-whistle effect; you may not be making noise about what you do, but the mad dogs in the neighborhood pick up on your vibe and come a-running en masse. Although the luck of the draw sometimes plopped me down next to some extraordinary personalities, like the Duchess of York, Sarah Ferguson (sweet, talkative, and remarkably candid), champion skater Kurt Browning (who actually recognized me from a Just For Laughs TV show I had just hosted), and Celine Dion (who slept . . . was it something I said?), most of my seatmates came in two varieties: comatose or frenzied, the latter far outweighing the former.

The epitome of the insufferable seatmate was a woman I met on a trip to Europe. Our paths initially crossed in the Air Canada first-class lounge in Toronto, where she introduced me to her husband. The two were fans of the festival and had once attended a conference at which I spoke. Nice meeting you—but it wasn't as simple as that. The woman deluged me with questions and was all too overjoyed when she discovered that we were on the same flight. Knowing that my seat was in a row of two, I thanked God that there was no chance the couple would be seated next to me.

As is my habit, I boarded the plane at the first call. I like to be settled, with a newspaper or laptop, as others stream through the aisles. That's also when I get to play Loto-Seat, a game in which I try to guess who my flying partner will be. Will it be the bold businessman, the attractive student, or the ever-popular mother-and-child combo?

"Well, it won't be her," I chuckled to myself as the yappy lady approached with her husband, checking their boarding passes. "Is this 1C?" she asked, pointing to the vacant cushion next to me. "Why, yes," I said, startled. Turning to her husband, she said, "See you later, honey." She kissed him goodbye, and he moved deeper into the bowels of the plane. My astonishment must have been obvious, because she then explained, "We only had one upgrade certificate." And next came the words that stung like a Sonny Liston crosshook: "And I'm so excited to sit next to you, because, you know, I can't sleep on a plane . . ." Delivering the knockout blow, she added, ". . . and I know *so many jokes!*"

Auuuuggggghhhhhh! A joke teller! There is no supercomputer strong enough to calculate how many times I've been accosted in restaurants, in hospitals, at parent-teacher meetings, and at funerals by well-meaning but overbearing people who bombard me with jokes I've heard at least twelve thousand times before, usually screwing up the punchline in the process, and culminate the experience by telling me, "You can use it if you want!"

I was trapped. Every other seat in the section was taken. The next flight was in twenty-four hours, and although that option was becoming more appealing by the second, I hung tough. The usual strategy for nullifying such verbal molestation is to flip open a book or start typing on a computer; people tend to get the message and direct their verbiage elsewhere, or, better still, turn it off. But with this woman my formerly foolproof tactic was about as effective as stopping a charging elephant with a flyswatter. Every effort I made to ignore her was counterbalanced by an increase in the vocal barrage.

At one point, out of desperation, in midsentence—politeness be damned!—I pulled on my headphones and cranked up the music full blast. Her reaction? She kept talking! Like a true artist who doesn't need the validation of an audience, her words kept pouring out. About an hour later, despite my attempts to laser-focus my eyes on my book (and let me tell you how tiring it can be to avoid all peripheral retinal movement), I couldn't help noticing that the woman was maniacally clicking her remote-control console, waving and jabbing it in the air. Disregard it! Be oblivious! Let someone else react! But it was no use. My sense of curiosity, mixed with my upbringing of empathy, got the better of me.

"Is something wrong?" I asked, removing my headphones. "This thing doesn't work," she complained. On most overseas flights, the business-class cabins are equipped with personal entertainment systems that allow you to choose from a catalog of video entertainment. Like your TV remote, the console changes channels, controls volume, and so on. I asked the lady what the problem was, but I shouldn't have.

"It doesn't change the channel," she grumbled.

"How can you tell?" I said, reaching into her arm rest to liberate her personal TV. "You don't even have your screen up."

She lit up. "Ohhhhhh, it's for *this!* I thought it was for *that*." She pointed to the projection screen at the front of the cabin.

"You mean, you thought, that *your* control controlled ..." I stopped myself and returned to my book. Take a deep breath. Relax. Ignore.

I must have a guardian angel, because my seatmate, exhausted from wagging her jaw and clicking her finger, finally fell asleep. Two hours of peace! But, upon waking, she left me one more verbal pearl to remember her by. As the plane banked towards its landing site in Germany, it passed over some of the lushest greenery these eyes have ever seen. It was sunrise, and the landscape was truly a sight to behold, so I didn't mind that the woman leaned over me to look out the window. She gazed for about five seconds. "Isn't it beautiful," she sighed. "The country that killed my parents!"

As crazy as things were when I was alone, the lunacy was compounded when I traveled with a colleague. In terms of fun on the road, one plus one indeed equaled three. Gilbert was the craziest. He was always late for the most outlandish reasons,[38] and his attention span at meetings was so short that you needed a stopwatch to measure it. In 1987 I set up a meeting with Schecter-Cone, a major PR firm; I was begging them to take us on as clients. Paul Burditch, a partner in the firm's L.A. office, flew to New York for the meeting, and he brought along the company's president and its main East Coast associates for a get-together at the swanky Russian Tea Room. We passed by big-time movers and shakers as we were ushered to one of the restaurant's main "power tables" (as per *Spy* magazine's on-the-money map of who sits where at the RTR).

Within minutes, Gilbert was on another planet. At least there he could do no harm. After about forty-five minutes, though, upon his reentry, is when he would get really dangerous. Forty-five minutes past the hour I felt a dribble on my thigh. Gilbert had smuggled his water glass under the table, and every time I spoke during the round-table conversation, he poured a little more water down my leg. Not only was this less than comfortable physically, but it would also make a huge pseudo pee stain on my pants, visible to all when I stood up.

Seeking immediate revenge, I loaded up my butter knife with a wad of yellow dairy. First showing it to my partner, I slowly moved it under the table. Gilbert was wearing a two-thousand-dollar Kenzo suit, and he was horrified. "It's only water," he whispered. "It's only water."

Don't forget that this psychodrama was being played out before the partners of a prestigious public relations firm, and, up until now, we'd pulled it off without them noticing a thing. I knew, though, that by buttering Gilbert's crotch I'd trigger a major detonation, and I didn't

---

[38] My favorite: flying to L.A., he was detained after airport security guards found huge knives in his briefcase; he'd taken them to his gourmet cooking course the previous evening and forgotten to remove them.

want to blow the meeting. So I returned the gooey knife to my plate and plotted another form of revenge.

In those early, low-budget days, Gilbert and I shared hotel rooms on the road. I was leaving later that afternoon, but Gilbert was staying on in New York for a few more days. After saying goodbye to all of my Russian Tea Room companions, I returned to the hotel to pack. And to settle the score. When Gilbert made his way back to the room later that night, he found a surprise waiting for him in the bathroom sink. Every pair of underwear and socks that he had with him—clean and dirty—was there, soaked and floating. On the mirror I'd scrawled a subtle message with a bar of soap: "It's only water!"[39]

Before Mark Goldman left Just For Laughs to start a successful spice and noodle business, he and I were frequent road warriors and roomies. Mark was the festival's director of finance, and he accompanied me on many a trip when TV deals were being negotiated. One such negotiation took place in London later in the fall of '87. At that time overseas flights out of Montreal left from Mirabel Airport, a monstrosity located about an hour out of town. You had to leave the city core over three hours before your departure time lest you be caught in a traffic jam and miss the flight. We often had two hours to kill before takeoff, and that left us with three options: shop duty free, beg for upgrades, or drink. Since I was never the greatest flier, the third option was always the most popular with me, especially if I'd been unsuccessful with the second.

Such was the case on one particular evening. Mark and I sat at the lounge bar, surveying people booked on our flight. We spotted one fifty-or-so-year-old guy, dressed in lederhosen and sporting a hunter's hat complete with upside-down brush, who kept talking to himself. What an oddball! An eyeball magnet—we couldn't stop looking at him. Not the friendliest of chaps, he later snapped "Behave!" at us while we were screwing around in the endless airport security lineup. Being a tad tipsy, we couldn't help but giggle like two schoolboys.

On the plane, our seats were positioned directly under the public address speakers, which were blasting at an inordinately high volume.

---

[39] Actually, it wasn't. I had mixed in a minibottle of hotel shampoo, as well.

Our heads had already begun to pound. To make matters worse, our flight path was Montreal-London-Düsseldorf, so every announcement—and there are scores of them on Air Canada—was repeated not only in the standard English and French, but also in German. After the sixth straight proclamation, Mark couldn't take anymore. "Enough with the German!" he moaned loudly. "And vhat is wrong mit German?" came an authoritative voice from behind us. It was the lederhosen guy! Once more, we'd pissed him off. "We better stay away from this guy," I told Mark.

Mealtime, more wine. Mark was getting increasingly silly. And all the liquid was taking its toll on me. "I gotta go to the bathroom, and you better stop screwing around by the time I get back," I jokingly warned. "Or, put another way—behave!" Mark cracked up. I knew he would do something dopey when I returned, so I was prepared for it. The cabin was darkened, but on my way back down the aisle I could still see Mark. What a goof! He was sitting there, seat straight up, with his blanket over his head. I didn't really understand the joke, but I guess he thought it was funny. Then I got it. He had moved over to take my window seat. Ho ho, what a card.

"Get out of my seat, you idiot," I said. He didn't move. "Okay, Mark, enough." I was giggling again, and I punched him in the shoulder. "All right, if that's what you want, I'll sit here," I relented, but not before whacking him hard on the head. Hmmm . . . his head felt funny. Different. I whipped off the blanket.

It was the German guy!

His bottom teeth ripped into his top lip; his eyes ripped fist-size holes right through me. I started to panic. "Oh my God," I blathered. "I'm sorry . . . I thought you were . . ."

Three rows ahead, looking back on this fine mess from our seats, was Mark—innocent, with no idea what was going on. I scampered back to him, and he was naturally inquisitive. "I'll tell you, but you have to promise you won't laugh," I said. "Promise?" Mark promised, and I told. He laughed so hard that the flight attendant ran over to see what was the matter. "I'll tell you," Mark said between gasps, "but you have to promise you won't laugh!"

For some strange reason, Germans and Germany have always

brought out the wurst in me. Okay, bad joke, but things were never dull for me in Deutschland. My wildest journey there was with André Picard, the former head of IMAX, who executive produced *The Rolling Stones at the Max* concert film. André was the head of our TV department for a few years, and at one point he'd wanted some help righting a deal that was going very wrong with a German TV network. We were to meet with Jacky Dreksler and Hugo Egon Balder, two major producers and our partners on the deal, at the WDR studios in Cologne.

I was coming from London, Picard from Paris, and I got there first. By now you should be able to guess what I did as soon as I arrived— yup, I went shopping. I asked the front-desk clerk, who was fluent in English, if there was a shopping area nearby. Luckily, or so I thought, there was one on the outskirts of town, about twenty minutes away, and the clerk called a cab for me. I didn't speak a word of German, but I still managed to buy a Steilmann sweater and enjoy a great lunch of marinated squid (hey, it's Germany!) at the shopping center. It was 4:00 P.M., and I had to meet Picard at 6:00; we were due at the studio by 6:30. I walked outside the small mall to the taxi stand.

But there was no taxi stand to be found anywhere around the shopping center. I did the whole tour twice. That seemed odd, but I did notice what I thought was a taxi stop further up the road, so I walked to it and waited. And waited. It became clear that I had a better chance of being picked up by the Mir Space Station than I did by a taxi at this stop. It was 4:30. "Maybe I'll have better luck flagging one down," I thought, so I stood in the middle of the busy road. Nothing even resembling a cab passed by. I tried hitchhiking with equally ineffective results. I waved frantically at buses, cop cars, kids on bikes, but to no avail. I had no idea where I was, except that I'd found my way into the middle of an industrial area of Cologne. I remembered that the taxi I'd taken from the hotel had crossed a bridge coming in, so—what else could I do?—I set out on foot to look for the nearest body of water. It was now 5:00 P.M.

I was scared. No cell phone, no change for a pay phone (which I wouldn't know how to use, anyway). I should've marked my trail with breadcrumbs. I kept walking.

At about 5:30 I came across what appeared to be a hotel. Unlike the Hyatt or the Hilton, European suburban hotels aren't monolithic structures with a concierge service and a huge staff. I was staying at the biggest and best place in town, and it only had about sixteen rooms. This little place I'd found was a combination bar/gas station/hotel, but to me it was the holy manger. Inside I encountered a lady who seemed to be covering everything. She greeted me, in German, from behind the bar. I said "Hello," but English apparently didn't register with her. She spoke to me again in German.

By now, the stress, the fatigue, and the fear were getting to me. I had to get back to my hotel, and fast. I don't know why I suddenly recalled a story Quebec comedian Michel Courtemanche had once told me, but, thankfully, I did. In a nutshell, when Michel did his first tour of Canada's Maritime provinces, he spoke no English. One day he'd desperately needed change, so he went into a corner store, strung together some vowels and consonants in a rhythm that sounded vaguely English-like, and added the word "change" at the end. The storekeeper replied, "Oh, you want some change?"; Michel nodded, and his mission was accomplished.

Now I desperately needed a taxi. Conjuring up some of my late grandmother's Yiddish, picking up pieces of John F. Kennedy's "Ich bin ein Berliner" speech, imitating Hitler's mob oratories, inspired by Courtemanche, I spewed out a stream of German-sounding nonsense before uttering the magic word: "Ich minsct lech chazen schtupp ocht mein veis mir ver ghargit . . . *taxi!*" Or something like that. It worked.

I suspect the woman asked me if I wanted a taxi, because I responded to what she said with "Ya! Ya!" and there was a cab waiting outside ten minutes later. I also suspect that she offered me a much-appreciated beer, because I responded "Ya! Ya!" to her next utterance, and she served me one. I left her a huge tip (I think) and climbed into perhaps the most beautiful mode of transportation I had ever seen. I had no idea where I was staying, what it was called, or where it was, but I showed the driver a matchbook I had taken from the front desk and let him figure it out for himself. Recalling some dialogue I'd learned from a particularly profound episode of *Hogan's Heroes*, I added, "Mach schnell!"

I got back to the hotel at 6:15, in time to see Picard flipping out—

pacing, flapping his arms, and swearing. Despite his fear of missing that important meeting, he was more worried that I was dead than pissed off that I was late. Another taxi was waiting to take us to the studio. I thanked my savior—the driver who'd just delivered me—one last time (I hope he understood "merci beaucoup"), jumped into the waiting cab with André, and we sped off. But wait. This one ain't over yet.

Hugo and Jacky weren't in the best of moods. They had a show to shoot that night, and here they were trying to patch up a contract dispute with production partners they had corresponded and conversed with but never met in person. Jacky was, shall we say, not exactly warm when we walked into his vast office. Hugo was busy putting out fires downstairs, and Jacky himself was busy dealing with other problems on the phone. He motioned to us to sit on a set of couches that formed a precision V (hey, it's Germany!) in front of a bank of TV monitors and VCRs. Exhausted from my ordeal, I plunked myself down. Picard did the pacing this time.

A cute little girl of about seven walked into the office and sat in front of the TV screens. She was Jacky's daughter, there to visit her daddy. I have a way with kids, even those whose language I don't speak, and after a few minutes of my parental foolishness she was laughing. Good political move. I took out my wallet, and, using the slow, loud, deliberate English North Americans use when speaking to those who don't understand the language, I showed her a picture of my son Aidan, who was about her age. Jacky, his phone call completed, came over, took the picture from my hand, and studied it. It was my son's official class photo from Hebrew Foundation School. He was wearing a telltale yarmulke.

Jacky raised his eyes from the photo. Then, like a World War II commandant, he said, menacingly, "You're a Jewwwww?" I glanced at Picard. Bald pate sweating, mouth open like an O, he looked like the figure in Edvard Munch's painting *The Scream*. I heard my heart thump. I felt my throat tighten. But, proudly, I spit out the words, "Yes, I am." Jacky went bananas.

"Me too! I can't believe it! Hugo and I are, like, the only Jews around here!" To Hugo, who'd just arrived, he called, "Hugo! Hugo! Come quick!

Another Jew! One of us!" I looked over at Picard again. He was dancing. To this day, he insists that he said, "It's a done deal!" But I still swear I heard him shout, "It's a miracle!"

My last travel tale has nothing to do with Germany but lots to do with miracles. It's a miracle I didn't get killed, or at least arrested, for a certain stunt that I pulled in October 1990. Marty Klein, who was always looking out for me, suggested that Bruce Hills and I attend a dinner being held at the Waldorf Astoria in New York in honor of MTV Networks Chairman Tom Freston. Tom was a dashing, Harrison Ford look-alike, and he and I had first met on a fiftieth-floor balcony at the Riviera Hotel in Las Vegas, where we discussed my acrophobia. Since then, Tom had brought Just For Laughs to MTV in the form of an annual half-hour special that Bruce produced for us, and, believe me, this was the least we could do in return.

Freston's fete was more than just another rubber-chicken-black-tie affair. It was called The Night of a Thousand Heroes, and the guest list was limited to one thousand people. The event featured live entertainment from Bonnie Raitt and Paul Simon, and, what's more, it was a high-end costume party—you were expected to dress up as some sort of, well, hero. I figured there would be five hundred Supermans and an equal number of Batmans, and you don't go to one of these things to blend into the crowd. After bending my brain to come up with something unique, I was hit by the obvious: Who are the stereotypical Canadian heroes? Mounties! Despite Bruce's reticence, I went out, scored two crimson Royal Canadian Mounted Police outfits, from felt hat to patent-leather spats, and prepared to do the Dudley Do-Right thing.

This was to be my last trip of the year, as my wife was expecting our second child in early November, and we had set Halloween as the travel cutoff date. As expected, The Night of a Thousand Heroes was a fine mélange of power schmoozing and howling at powerful people in goofy costumes. Sitting with Bruce and I was an editor of *Variety* and Paul Jabara, actor and writer of the camp classic "It's Raining Men." We had a blast.

Eventually, however, all good things must come to an end, and this one did fairly early. It wasn't even 11:00 P.M. when the room emptied (quite a sight to see drunken people in wild getups parading through the prim, opulent Waldorf lobby), and I was somewhat disappointed. My flight left at 3:00 the next afternoon, and, since this would be my last night out for a while, I wasn't going to let my costume go to waste. I suggested that we make an appearance at Columbus, a popular industry hangout on Columbus Avenue and an after-hours haunt of everyone from Danny Aiello, Dana Carvey, and Jerry Seinfeld to Mason Reese, the redheaded kid from the Underwood deviled ham commercial. No way, said Bruce. Fun, yes, but potentially damaging to our professional image. "Let's go where nobody knows us," he suggested.

Ten minutes later, Bruce and I were in a cab heading towards 42nd Street. Now in 1990, this famous thoroughfare was not the war zone it was in the sixties and seventies, but it was still a far cry from the sterilized, Walt Disneyfied family zone it is today. The taxi driver, noting our rather unconventional garments, asked who we were. "Canadian military," Bruce responded with Teutonic seriousness. It was the time of Operation Desert Storm, so I followed up by playing the patriot card. "We're shipping out tomorrow to bolster the American military operation in the Gulf," I added in a monotone. The cabbie was incredulous.

"You're helping our boys?"

"Yes we are, sir."

He stopped the cab and turned around to face us: "Then you don't pay!"

Bingo! We had hit the motherlode. From that point on, it was a challenge to see how far we could exploit this masquerade. First stop, fast-food joint. We weren't hungry, but we ordered coffee and muffins. Same questions. Same answers. Same basic result—this time, free eats. "I saw a jacket I wanted this afternoon," I reflected. "I wonder if I could have scammed that for free. Jeez, too bad the stores are closed." But the clubs weren't, most notably Show World, a famous nightspot of ill repute on 42nd Street and 8th Avenue. Next stop!

While we were no Margaret Meads, we did make an amazing anthropological/social-psychological discovery that night: The scummier people are, the more respectful they are of Canadian law enforcement. (It had to be that, because they certainly weren't intimidated by my five-foot-four-inch frame.) Case in point was the reaction we received at Show World, home of strippers, transsexuals, degenerates, live sex shows, and worse. The club's management and staff had seen it all many times over, so we figured they'd treat us as a couple of sickos with a red fetish. Instead, we were treated like heroes and offered a smorgasbord of smut—all for free. "You guys are helping our boys? You guys gonna kick some Iraqi ass?" they asked. "Here, take this magazine. You'll need it out there. You gotta video machine on the boat? Take these videos!"

Then came the whisper. "Listen," a bearded boss told me, "go into a booth, and I'll send in any girl you want on the other side of the glass. It's on me."

"What am I supposed to do there?" I asked sternly.

"Jerk off," the guy replied.

"Sorry, sir," I said soberly. "As much as I appreciate your kind offer, military regulations dictate that no part of my uniform be removed in a public locale."

"Oh, no problem!" he replied defensively. "Just trying to help out."

"So are we sir, so are we."

By 2:00 A.M. the novelty was wearing thin, and the thick mustache I was wearing was itching me to death. We left the hospitable Show World to farewell waves and whoops of "Kick some butt!" "Thanks for being there for us!" and "Be careful!"

Bruce and I were still howling at 2:30, when we got back to our room at the Mayflower Hotel. Our hilarity was interrupted, though, when the phone rang. Our minds started racing paranoiacally. Who could be calling at this hour? Maybe the guys at the club had found out we were phonies and followed us back here to kill us! Maybe someone had reported us and it was the FBI calling—the penalties for impersonating a police officer can be extreme! Maybe Freston had seen us and wanted to cancel our show! Cautiously, I lifted the receiver. "Andrew?" It was Lynn, my wife. "My water just broke. When's the next flight?"

The next flight wasn't for hours, but I still took off for LaGuardia—in full Mountie regalia—right away. The Montreal flight was at 7:00 A.M., on the old Eastern Airlines, and the wait for it was the longest four hours of my life. The airport bathrooms were locked until 6:00 A.M. to discourage drug use and other undesirable activities, so I couldn't change until then. I sat in a corner, reading, trying to look inconspicuous (yeah, right), but I was still bugged by transients throughout the night.

"Get out of here before I arrest you," I told them. It worked on most. One cocky guy, however, was a little wiser than that. "You're Canadian," he slurred. "You have no authority here." I growled back, "Try me, mofo. Make my day."

After about six more hours, my day *was* made. That's when Lynn, after holding out until my plane had landed and my cab had delivered me to the delivery room, gave birth to our son Hayes Brody. Finally, I was off the road. Until November, at least.

UNCLE MILTIE

To help advance the Just For Laughs Museum concept, we decided to launch the Humor Hall of Fame in 1991, a full two years before the museum complex's planned opening. Our timing wasn't exactly ideal. We had no building, just a gutted shell filled with dirt. We had no board of directors. We had no voting system. We didn't even have any selection criteria. But why should we let a few minor details like those stop us?

What we did have was a New York-based publicist named Glenn Schwartz, who, in turn, had a client named Milton Berle. They were a strange couple, Glenn being more than a half-century younger than the eighty-three-year-old Milton. Yet Glenn worked his butt off for Milton, and in the somewhat manufactured honor we were offering he actually smelled mucho media opportunities for his client. All three parties—Just For Laughs, Glenn, and Milton—had something to gain by pulling this one off. Although he was unquestionably a comedy pioneer, Milton's best years were behind him; the festival could do a lot worse than having North America's first TV star as the inaugural inductee for its Hall of Fame; and Glenn could kill two birds (charge two clients) with one stone.

Glenn set up the pitch meeting on a weekday afternoon at the Los Angeles Friar's Club, Milton's legendary haunt, clubhouse, and office. Unlike its more bustling New York counterpart (seen in films like *The*

Sunshine Boys and *King of Comedy*), the L.A. Friar's Club was a dreary place, tucked into a nondescript white stucco corner building on Little Santa Monica Boulevard. On the afternoon of our meeting only a handful of sundry staff members were shuffling about; there were no other customers to be seen as Glenn and I double-teamed Uncle Miltie on his home turf.

Naturally, I came equipped with a full festival promo package, and, in a rather over-the-top sales pitch, I outlined all the benefits Milton would derive from agreeing to accept the honor. The adulation! The trophy! All seen—hold on to your hairpiece—*live* on the Showtime television network! But trying to get Milton excited about winning another award was like trying to get a hooker excited about turning another trick. "I don't know where I'd put the damn thing," he grinned. "Maybe I'll throw out an Emmy."

Despite the reality of the times, in Milton's mind he was still the world's biggest star. Being one small part of a TV special on a cable network wasn't exactly the greatest turn-on to a man who had been anointed "Mr. Television" by the Academy of Television Arts and Sciences. He knew we were the ones riding his coattails—and doing so for a fee that I still can't believe I had the balls to offer.

To this day I have no idea what the turning point was in this seemingly futile negotiation (perhaps it was Glenn's preposterous pledge that Montreal would change the name of Milton Street to Milton Berle Street in his honor), but, after enduring an hour of so of my pleading, Milton simply turned to Glenn and asked, "So, should I do it?" When Glenn answered in the affirmative, we had a deal, we had an inductee, and we had a Hall of Fame. Well, at least on paper.

For a less-than-whopping $25,000, Milton would make three appearances at the St. Denis Theater. On Friday and Saturday he would perform a brief five-minute set (keep that number in mind—it's going to be important later) as part of the Showtime show and be presented with the Hall of Fame award by host Mary Tyler Moore. On Sunday, after the Showtime show had already aired, Milton would host an entire gala show himself. The conditions Milton requested for this appearance were far from extraordinary: two first-class flights, the hotel's best suite, all meals paid, and the guarantee that he would be promoted, and always remembered, as the first person ever inducted into the Just For Laughs Hall of Fame. Piece of cake. I've had mimes from Germany demand more.

Somehow, it all seemed too easy, especially considering that in his heyday Milton was feared and loathed for being the most demanding, obsessive control freak in show business. The pacing on his *Texaco Star Theater* show was purported to have beem ruled by an applause-milking device known as "the Berle light"; God forbid that anyone should deliver his or her line before or after the precise millisecond that the light faded to black. His micromanaging style didn't mellow as he aged, either. Just For Laughs staffers like set designer Leo Yoshimura, who also toiled for *Saturday Night Live*, told horror stories of how Milton had terrorized everyone from the lighting director to the coffee boy when he hosted *SNL* in April 1979. To this day, the legend goes, Milton's *SNL* appearance is the only one that producer Lorne Michaels has ever banned from being rebroadcast. So, were we experiencing the calm before the storm? Or was I just being paranoid? On Friday, July 19, at the dress rehearsal for the Showtime live show, we'd know for sure.

Milton showed up at the theater in fine spirits for the afternoon run-through, and he appeared genuinely touched by the tribute assembled by Bob Kaminsky, the show's producer. Kaminsky knew how to deal with old timers; his father had been a writer for the equally overbearing Jackie Gleason. Over and above the standard video-clip package of Milton's career highlights (including some mighty cool footage of duets with Elvis and Frank Sinatra), Kaminsky had mounted a live re-creation of the *Texaco Star Theater* opening, complete with singing mechanics in full grease-monkey garb.

No complaints, no histrionics, no fuss. In fact, the only thing remotely out of the ordinary was a request Milton made to Willie Mercer, our head of backstage talent relations that year. And I quote:

Willie: "Mr. Berle, can I get you anything?"

Milton: "Yeah, a girl to suck my cock."

Willie: "Uh, let me see what I can do."[40]

---

[40] Willie, being the fine, upstanding orthodox Jew that he is, blushed and brought Milton flowers, instead.

Some of you more informed readers were perhaps waiting for this moment—when the subject of Milton's mythical schlong (rumored to be one of the longest ever seen in the human species) was finally, pardon the pun, brought up. Leo Yoshimura recalled that on the *Saturday Night Live* set anybody who asked was treated to a glimpse; many who didn't were, as well. At Just For Laughs, I'm somewhat disappointed to say, the monster remained quietly locked away. When its master was in public, anyway.

His penis and his emotions seemingly on the same mellow wavelength, Milton took to the stage for his tribute at approximately 10:30 P.M. Thus began one of the most bizarre episodes in Just For Laughs history. The mere sight of him walking through the curtain flanked by two green festival mascots sparked a spontaneous standing ovation. "Oh this is a *gooood* audience," he cooed. "I'll be on for three hours."

Cut to the crowded backstage corridor. All of a sudden someone threw a twenty-dollar bill onto the catering table and barked, "Twelve minutes." Apparently, "going long" is not a condition that applied exclusively to Milton's prodigious member. I quickly learned that his reputation was to ignore limits and perform to his heart's content, no matter how much time had been allotted to him. The Hollywood execs who were gathered behind the scenes knew this, and they were about to make the most of it.

It still amazes me how fast it all came together, that backstage betting parlor. Before I could even gasp, there was a tote board; names, numbers, and money were flying faster in that cramped corridor than they did on Wall Street during a panicky late Friday afternoon. An agent with a chronograph Breitling was the official timekeeper, and all bets were on.

"Twenty bucks on 15:05!"

"Put ten on 11:48 and ten more on 12:17!"

"What's the max? I want 10:34!"

During this madness, Mary Tyler Moore emerged from her dressing room; it was almost time for her to go onstage and present Milton with the award, so she had to be positioned. Mary was always the picture of elegance, and I thought she would be repulsed by the frenzy that greeted her, but as she was being touched up in the wings her husband,

Dr. Robert Levine, came over to us and said, "What times are still available? Mary wants to bet twenty dollars."

Even noisier than the delirious betting was the losing. The longer Milton continued, the more people dropped off. With every tick of the Breitling, some ponytailed Hollywood type, some technician, or some other act waiting to go onstage would be out of the money and would bemoan the fact loudly. It was the Luxor Stakes all over again. When Milton finally bowed out, over fourteen minutes had elapsed, and an agent from APA raked in over three hundred dollars (his ecstatic reaction was so rowdy that you'd think he'd won a major lottery). On Saturday night, during the live-live show, the backstage scene was repeated and Richard Belzer emerged victorious with a time of 11:11. Apparently, Milton's first words upon coming off stage that night were, "Who won?"

So far Milton had been irreverent and surreal—but not tempestuous. For that we would have to wait until the following day. The weight of the live TV show lifted from my shoulders, I left the Sunday gala in the very capable hands of Bruce Hills. We always considered Sunday's event to be the "slack" gala, and the micromanaging and hand-holding of the previous TV-oriented shows weren't usually needed. My plan was to carouse very late at the Showtime wrap party (which involved as much political posturing with the network execs for next year as it did celebrating) and sleep in. Then, fully refreshed, I would arrive at the theater in the midafternoon, after Bruce had put all the other comedians through their paces, just in time to walk Milton through his.

It was almost 5:00 A.M. when I made it back to the hotel, drained but happy and relaxed. I put a "do not disturb" on my phone, closed my cellular, and drifted drunkenly into la-la-land. I woke the next day at about 2:00 P.M. For some strange reason, I took the cell phone into the bathroom with me and left it near the sink as I showered. For some even stranger reason, I turned it on as soon as I stepped out of said shower. Once again, trouble made the phone ring even before the "on" button was fully depressed. It was Bruce. Over and over, like a mantra, he shouted the following three phrases, each time emphasizing a different word: "They're going mental!" "Get here now!" "They're gonna quit!"

Soaking wet, I threw on last night's clothes and sped over to the St. Denis. To this day, the vision that greeted me haunts my thoughts.

There, on the stage, was Milton, still wearing the trench coat he'd arrived in, pointing at the band and barking orders at the poor sap on drums. "That's not how to do a drumroll!" he bellowed. He proceeded to explain, in great detail, the mechanics of a musical walk-on. "Put a button on it!"

Bruce and Babar Monfette, the stage manager that year, swooped down on me like vultures on a filet mignon. Milton, they informed me, had showed up early, taken over the rehearsals, and backed up the whole process. After three hours they were still working out the simple walk-on of the night's first act, England's Jo Brand, and Milton was obsessing over the drumroll that would cap off the band's musical intro. Jo, a dark and sour personality at the best of times, was livid. I smiled weakly and said hello to her. "Get him off, or I'll kill both of you," she snarled. I turned to Babar for consolation. "Get him off, or my whole crew is quitting," he threatened, making Jo Brand sound like Mother Teresa.

I looked into the wings and saw an exhausted, frustrated stage crew. I looked into the audience and saw a backlog of glum, bored comedians. Sitting among them was the only chipper soul in the house— Bill Brioux, a *TV Guide* writer to whom I had promised a five-minute interview with Milton sometime during rehearsal. Yeah, and this was the "slack" gala.

I walked over to Milton, and we exchanged pleasantries.

"Listen," he whispered softly in my ear. "Your drummer is a piece of shit. But I'm working with him. I think we're almost there."

"Milton, maybe we should just move this along," I appealed to him subtly. "I think that the comedians are getting a little upset."

Just then, the insolent Chris Lynam, he of "Roman candle up the ass" fame, called out from his seat, "C'mon! Get off the stage, you old fuck!" Milton turned to him, squinted, and turned back to me. I shuddered at what was coming.

"Listen to that," he beamed. "They love me, these kids!"

Babar. Brand. Berle. Boy oh boy, this was a lose-lose situation. But then—drumroll please—I experienced divine inspiration. I ran to Paul Coderre, the lighting director, and told him to close all the lights onstage. Click. Pitch black. "What the hell's going on?" Milton shouted.

"Three o'clock!" I cried, pointing to my watch as I trotted back onstage. "Union break! Everyone off the stage!"

The house was nonunion and so was the crew. Everyone just stared at me in bewilderment. But Milton, respectful of theatrical traditions, turned and walked quietly into the wings. As Bruce led him towards his dressing room, I sped over to Bill Brioux. "Bill, remember I promised you five minutes with Milton?" Brioux nodded appreciatively. "Well, I lied. You've got four hours. Whatever you do, don't let him out of there!"

With Milton safely imprisoned in his dressing room by Brioux's tape recorder, we switched on the lights and ran the rehearsal in double-time, with yours truly substituting for the legend on performer intro-ductions and callbacks. And, at 7:00, just as the doors of the theater were being opened to the public, Bruce and I went to see Milton in his dressing room. "Thirty minutes to curtain, Mr. Berle!" He got up, thanked a haggard Brioux, and calmly put on his tux. After applying a dab of black shoe polish to cover up his bald spot, Milton took to the stage and pulled off the show effortlessly. He didn't complain about the opening drumroll and was gracious to all the other performers, with the notable exception of Richard Belzer, whom he called "Charlie" for some unknown reason.

When it was all over, including the obligatory posing for backstage photos with Bruce, Kaminsky, and me, Milton asked to borrow my cell phone. "He's gotta call his bookie in L.A.," Glenn explained. "Go to the party, I'll bring it to you there." As I boarded the bus to take me to the waterfront closing festivities, I couldn't help thinking about the conver-sation Milton was having at that very moment. "Guess what? Made 'em wait over three hours!" I imagined him saying. "So, tell me, who had 3:07:42, and how much did they put down?"

KILL OR BE KILLED

Much has been written about comedy's strangely sadistic/masochistic terminology: comics who do well "kill," "destroy," or "murder" an audience; those who do poorly "die," "stiff," or "bomb." While showbiz in general is inherently confrontational, its ostensibly easygoing comedy division is the most vicious. Don't let the smiles fool you—comedy is not a business for the faint of heart. The meek shall not inherit the mirth.

To borrow a line from comic-beater Bernard Fredette, I am not a violent man. However, in order to survive a decade and a half in the comedy biz, I've been obliged to wield wicked weaponry in more than my fair share of blood-spilling battles. More often than not, my own injuries were far more grievous than those of my opponents, but the business of show is not a winner-take-all game. Sometimes you've gotta take one for the team.

I don't want to bite the hand that fed me, but the TV networks were among the most cutthroat of my combatants. Although they'll put more money in your pocket than anyone else, don't expect there to be any left over once they're through with you. If they buy your show for $1,000,000, they want to see at least $1,500,000 of it on the screen. "Why, that's impossible!" you say. Yeah, go tell the networks that. And bring lots of Kleenex. Make no mistake about it, they're the ones holding the big end of the stick almost all of the time. And they're not afraid to swing it. Hard. To wit, a meeting I had with Showtime programming VP Jay Larkin, during which we discussed the lineup for our 1991 special.

"You better hit a home run with the show," he warned, "or else we may not be back at the ballpark next year."

I looked at him smugly. "But Jay, we have a three-year contract!"

He raised his index finger and pointed upward. "Look up. What do you see?"

"The ceiling?"

"Right. And you know who's sitting above that ceiling? About a hundred lawyers. They're waiting for me to give them something to do. If I say we have no three-year contract, they're gonna back *me* up, not *you*, kapish?

Gulp. And this was friend, not foe. No wonder Jay's now the guy who negotiates the network's boxing deals with genteel souls like Don King and Mike Tyson (and who threatened to whup the ass of Polish boxer Andrew Golota after his insipid performance ruined a lucrative pay-per-view telecast). Thanks to Jay, I learned yet another valuable lesson: "Breathe easy, and it'll be the last breath you'll ever take."

The networks were pussycats compared to the government, though. I was on the front line for a take-no-prisoners confrontation between the feds and the festival's major sponsor, which happened to be a tobacco company. This brawl featured Cold War-type propaganda, threats, counterthreats, intelligence reports, and name-calling, face-to-face altercations. Truth be told, I'm a fervent antismoker. I hate tobacco; but, as CEO of Just For Laughs, I hated the prospect of losing a million-dollar-a-year sponsor even more. It was a divisive fracas that lasted two years.

I could go on for days about political minefields or corporate terrorism, but I have a sneaking suspicion that your interest may lie elsewhere, in other types of festival war stories—likely those of the celebrity-smackdown variety, stuffed with larger-than-life personalities, explosive egos, and heavy artillery. So, let me pin on my Purple Heart, pull up an easy chair, and regale you.

STEVE ALLEN

I never met a human being as meticulous as Steve Allen. In fact, I never met a machine as meticulous as Steve Allen. He was the only man in the world who could make Bruce Hills seem laissez-faire. Obviously brilliant, Steve created and hosted *The Tonight Show*, and gave new meaning to the word prolific by writing thousands of songs and dozens of books.

And hundreds of pages of instructions.

Steve had exhaustive, single-spaced instruction sheets for just about every aspect of his performance; eleven pages on his stage setup, three pages on how to distribute cards for his question-and-answer routine, three more on how to stock his hotel room. Most artists had a rider; Steve had a Time-Life book series. What's more, all of his notes were composed in an uncompromising, somewhat patronizing tone. This, for example, is how he outlined (through an assistant) his simple nourishment requirements:

> Mr. Allen prefers *fresh-squeezed* fruit juices—orange juice,* grape juice—and perhaps a supply of apples, bananas, oranges, that sort of thing (enough to last the # of days of his stay). Also, please make sure it's in his suite when he arrives, not sent up hours later, as *sometimes happens.*
>
> *Special Note:* As may have already come to your attention, there has been a serious collapse of efficiency in America across the board in recent years. We see this reflected in Mr. Allen's personal experience, particularly when he travels. For example, the simple instructions above—having fruit juice and fruit available in his hotel room when he arrives—has, in recent years, only rarely been properly attended to. At the risk of sounding dramatic, therefore, I must emphasize the *importance* of this detail.
>
> Accordingly, it will be necessary for you—or someone you designate—to personally *supervise* this one detail. This means, obviously, that the hotel management office will have to be called—on the day of Mr. Allen's arrival—to make sure that more than one person on the hotel staff is assuming personal responsibility for following up this simple enough instruction.

If there is the slightest question in your mind about this, please feel free to discuss the matter with me by phone. Naturally, neither Mr. Allen—nor any other entertainer—ought to have to be personally concerned about making inquiries about such things when he arrives in your city, so I would really appreciate it if you could just arrange to have the juice and fruit waiting in his room, the way it was for many years. Thanks for your attention to this detail.

*I know that Mr. Allen is *not* particularly fond of orange juice made from concentrate. If they have only that kind of orange juice in your town, well, of course, I'm sure he'd rather have that than none at all. But you can get real juice just about any place these days, so please do that if you can, and buy the concentrate type only as a last resort. *Thank you!*

Whew! And that's the edited version. Needless to say, this was a man who knew what he wanted. Exactly what he wanted. Ambiguity had no place in the life of Steve Allen, which is exactly why our 1988 run-in was so volatile.

But, first, a little background to set the scene. It was Thursday, July 21, and Steve was hosting our gala show, doing his usual fine, thorough job. The night before there had been a postgala party at the Delta Hotel, which had degenerated into a minor scandal when attendees—festival artists and VIPs—were handed bills for the food and drink they'd consumed. We had another party scheduled after the show that Allen was hosting, and, to avoid any further tarnishing of our image, Gilbert and I had decided to pick up the tab for the whole thing, whatever it cost. To ensure that all of our performers and industry guests got the message, we printed up loud flyers announcing the party and the no-pay policy, then strategically placed one in every St. Denis Theater dressing room just after intermission.

I was backstage on Thursday night when, after an inspired performance by one of the gala acts, Steve returned to the stage, sat at his piano, and proudly proclaimed: "I was just handed this note backstage, from whom I have no idea." He brandished and displayed the flyer. "It says, 'Let's all get together after the show. There's a party at Club Jodees.'" After letting this sink in for a second, the delighted crowd applauded merrily. "You know where that is?" Steve inquired, looking at the front row. Then he dropped the big one: "Everybody's welcome and the food is free!"

The place went nuts. Hearing Steve say the words "Let's all get together after the show" had stopped me in my tracks. Now, hearing the jubilation chorus ringing throughout the theater, I was flabbergasted. As Steve returned to his dressing room, I followed in hot pursuit.

"Mr. Allen, there's been a terrible mistake," I explained impatiently when I caught up with him. "The note you just read onstage was for staff and artists only! It wasn't meant for the public!"

"Well someone would've had to tell me that for me to know," he defended himself, oh-so-rationally. "It was handed to me. I assumed it was an announcement you wanted made."

"Mr. Allen, right now I have 2,300 people expecting to come to a private party at a club that can hold, at most, 200!" I cried, visions of bankruptcy running through my head.

"Well, that's too bad. What do you want me to do about it?"

"I want you to go back and tell them you made a mistake!"

Steve stiffened. This breach of attention to detail was mine, not his. "No way," he said. "There is no way I can do that. You see, the mood in the room is high. If I go out there and tell them, that will kill the show."

"If you don't, there's gonna be a riot later."

"Sorry," he said flatly. "If I tell them about this error, they will turn on me."

"I promise you they won't," I beseeched. "They'll realize it's just a mistake. I promise you, they'll be fine."

After a few more minutes of arguing back and forth, Steve reluctantly agreed to set the record straight. Following the next performer, as promised, he clarified the situation and deinvited the crowd. Their mature, compassionate reaction? They booed. Long and loud. Steve chuckled onstage, but he was incensed once he got off. He didn't say anything to me for the rest of the evening, but he threw me many "I told you so" glances.

I figured I'd drown my sorrows at the party, but it proved to be no picnic, either. I spent most of the night playing bouncer outside Club

Jodees on Drummond Street, turning away a continuous flow of people, all of them protesting, "But Steve Allen invited me!"

MORT SAHL

In 1987 we inaugurated the concept of the Just For Laughs theme show. One Club Soda show we put together that year featured a slate of raunchy comedians (including Chris Rock, the masked Crusher Comic, and X-rated songsters MacLean and MacLean), so I called it The Nasty Show and tagged it with the line, "For adults only!" When it sold out in two days, I knew we were on to something (these days, The Nasty Show sells out twelve performances in a heartbeat).

By 1990 we had developed three more of these target-marketed thematic minigalas, in which a host and three or four acts would wax wittily about one specific subject. Into the mix went Jenny Jones's Girls Night Out, Bill Lee's The Comedy of Sports, and—the one we were highest on—The Comedy of Politics. The latter show featured Will Durst, Great Britain's acerbic Jeremy Hardy, and South African antiapartheid activist Pieter-Dirk Uys, but its main attraction was Mort Sahl.

In the realm of political satire, Sahl was the dean. His credentials extended from his days as a John F. Kennedy speechwriter to his recent one-man-show run on Broadway. While many felt that in 1990 his best years were behind him, I was ecstatic that I had managed to lure such a wily vet into the fold. We iced the deal at the La Scala restaurant in Beverly Hills, with Sahl's agent, Irvin Arthur, and Mort himself present. Although I loved and trusted Irvin—a Hollywood old-timer for whom Joan Rivers once toiled as a secretary—I wanted Mort at that meeting so that he could hear about the show, its concept, and its other participants straight from the horse's mouth. After an hour or so of whinnying, we shook hands with a, "See you at the festival."

Knowing that the subject matter of The Comedy of Politics was the antithesis of the lowbrow, popular stuff that fueled events like The Nasty Show, I instituted a one-hundred-percent refund policy to encourage people to take a chance on something a bit cerebral. "If, for any reason, you're not satisfied with The Comedy of Politics," the ads read, "we'll give you your money back with no questions asked." The last thing I wanted was to have Sahl play to a room that was anything less than full.

Sahl arrived in Montreal with his son on Wednesday, July 11, at 10:51 P.M. His stay proved to be the shortest of any performer in Just For Laughs history.

And the calls just kept on coming! First came the complaint about the flight. "Food was awful," said Mort. Next problem, his hotel room. "You call this a suite?" he demanded. There was more. Mort didn't like the fact that he was "sharing the bill with a bunch of nobodies." And he saw the money-back guarantee I'd offered as an insult, not a marketing tool. Then, the straw that broke the camel's back: we introduced Mort to Club Soda.

Because it boasted a roomy stage that brought performers close to all 450 people in the room, Club Soda had become one of the favorite comedy venues on the continent; comics just loved to perform there. At night, filled with fans, the stage area fully lit, speakers pumping out fun, it was magical. During the afternoon, beer-soaked, barren, and silent, it was, shall we say, no Broadway theater. But a pro should understand that. Mort didn't.

He arrived at 2:30 on Thursday afternoon, about half an hour late for his rehearsal. He looked around apprehensively and asked for the stage lights to be illuminated. When told that the technical director had just run across the street to pick up some Kentucky Fried Chicken, Mort decided that this was the last indignity he would suffer. To the shock of John Oakley, who was overseeing the show for us, Mort picked up, hailed a cab, and hightailed it back to the airport and to California.

I couldn't believe it when Oakley called to break the news. I dialed Irvin Arthur and went ballistic. Irvin played the game for his client.

"He didn't know there were other people on the bill," Irvin ventured.

"Bullshit!" I screamed. "You were there! You heard me explain the show, step by step!"

"He didn't feel treated right," Irvin parried.

"Horseshit!" I said, thinking of what farm animal's excrement I could use next. "He flew first class! He had a massive suite! We gave him Oakley as a personal assistant!"

"What can I tell you," Irvin sighed, exasperated. "He's a legend. He was on the cover of *Time* magazine!"

"So was Hitler!" I bellowed, before hanging up.

I was doomed. The show was starting in less than five hours, its star was on a plane back to L.A., and I was offering a money-back guarantee. Amazingly, though, that night only about forty people asked for a refund upon being informed of Mort's vanishing act. We reduced refunds to zero by the show's closing night. Better, still, the fact that we didn't have to cover Mort's bloated paycheck reduced the cost of the show, making it ultimately profitable. And, we learned one more important lesson: A strong concept can be a bigger star than a star. Best of all, though, Mort's desertion became a great running gag, dominating all festival conversation until Friday, when it was overshadowed—how stunningly apt—by Chris Lynam's red-hot anus.

WEIRD AL'S DANCING POTATOES

I often likened Just For Laughs to a dumptruck filled with sensitive explosives rolling brakeless down a pothole-pocked hill. With your hands taped to the steering wheel, the challenge would be to guide the truck down the incline without making the whole thing blow up in your face. There were always bumps, and explosions of varying degrees, but they usually occurred within the time frame of the festival. In 1990 we had one major explosion that went off weeks after the event was over.

It all started on Wednesday, July 18, during rehearsals for the Weird Al Yankovic gala, which was scheduled for that evening. For a song called "Addicted to Spuds," a parody of Robert Palmer's sexy "Addicted to Love," Al's manager, Jay Levey, asked me to find two female models who would don giant, guitar-holding potato costumes. Since the costumes would cover the models' entire bodies from the waist up, Levey's only requirements were that they have great legs and a half-decent sense of rhythm.

Levey had given me such short notice that I asked one of our backstage runners (who had lots of modeling experience) if she would do it for fifty dollars. Not only did she agree, but she also said that she had a friend who could fill the other potato suit for the same fee. Excellent! Deal done in five minutes. There was only one slight problem—it was too late to issue the girls' checks that day, but they'd be ready for pickup at the office by Friday. No problem. The role wasn't too demanding, but the slender-gammed girls were great at sashaying to the beat. The show ended, the festival ended, and all was right with the world. For a few weeks.

August was always the slowest month at Just For Laughs. It was indeed the calm after the storm, as tired, zombie-paced office staffers stumbled into work late to clean up and tie up loose ends. One day, the tranquility of our workplace was ruptured by a ranting madwoman. She burst in, shrieking, "I am the mother of the potato, and I want my daughter's money!"

Had I been there to hear this seemingly nonsensical rambling, I could've easily cracked the crackpot's code. However, I was sequestered on the third floor of the festival's new, three-story brownstone; the accountants and the administration staff who populated the ground floor had to deal with the situation on their own. They panicked, called 911, and reported that they were under attack by some sort of insane terrorist. As they screamed and hid under desks, the woman continued her tirade: "I am the mother of the potato, and I want my daughter's money!"

Within seconds, the police arrived. Hearing the commotion, I made my way downstairs, and there I witnessed some of the wildest repartee in Just For Laughs history. The woman thought that we had stiffed her daughter. In reality, the absentminded dancer had merely forgotten my instructions and had never come to pick up her check.

"So why didn't you just call, you lunatic!" Judith Suissa, our no-holds-barred head accountant barked at the enraged mother. "I had her check in my drawer!"

"Quiet, you," the woman barked back. "My daughter is underage. I'll sue you for hiring a minor!"

"Since when are there age requirements for vegetables?" Judith shot back.

The police got the check from Judith, gave it to the woman, and sent her on her way. But for weeks, I couldn't live down what was now referred to as "Spud Day Afternoon"—I had become inextricably linked with Ms. Potato Head. "I heard you got her pregnant and she gave birth to french fries," Judith razzed. "You deal with her mother when she comes looking for child support!"

MARCEL MARCEAU

He was the living definition of mime. I was a twenty-eight-year-old punk who was producing his first major TV special. Heading towards each other on a collision course, we became involved in a high-stakes game of chicken. Who would be the first to jump off? The answer will surprise you.

In 1988, we booked Marcel Marceau for a rare concert appearance in Montreal as part of the festival. To help amortize our costs, and to expose more people to his inimitable artistry, we added Marceau to the lineups of both our French and English galas. And, as a further tribute, we also included him in our HBO special. Host John Candy was thrilled when he heard the news.

Everything went perfectly on the French side. Showcasing routines from his more than forty years in the limelight, Marceau was showered with adulation. While his act was a little slow for some people's taste, most felt that seeing him live was a treat. Unfortunately, that treat would not be shared by our English audience. At the rehearsal for the English show, Marceau was appalled to see that the stage he had performed on earlier in the week had been altered to accommodate Leo Yoshimura's elaborate HBO set, which included a majestic checkerboard square at centerstage, a platform that was not only cut into the floor, but also rose above it by about a quarter-inch.

This diminutive elevation may seem like nothing to you or me, but to Marceau's sensitive steps of silence it was Mount Everest. And he wasn't willing to climb it.

"To perform, I need it to be level," he explained, calmly at first. "Why don't you just remove it?"

"I'm so sorry, Mr. Marceau," I said, "but I can't. It's a big part of our television 'look.'"

"So, why not keep it there for others but remove it for me?"

"It's not portable. There'd be a huge hole underneath. But, really, it's no big deal; the Institut de Jonglage (a France-based, highly-mobile juggling team) performed on it with no problem!"

Oops. Bad association. Comparing the man whose name is synonymous with silent expression to a bunch of jugglers was like comparing a fine French champagne to a Bartles & James wine cooler. I had touched a raw nerve. "They may have, but I won't," said Marceau, turning to leave. Before he went out the door, he looked back and snarled, "This is an outrage!"

I couldn't fathom what had just occurred. I had basically booted the great Marcel Marceau off a stage. Although I later did my best to bring him back, there was to be no compromise, no negotiation. He was gone forever. To this day I'm embarrassed about the result of our confrontation, but that cloud did have a silver lining. How many other people can say that Marcel Marceau, the Sultan of Shhhhh, actually raised his voice to them?

DON RICKLES AND WILLIAM SHATNER

Talk about odd couples. What could these two polar opposites possibly have in common? (Okay, besides the hair.) Would you believe, my left cheek? This will all make sense soon . . .

Don Rickles was booked to host a Just For Laughs gala on Thursday, July 23, 1998. I always made it a point to meet any host in advance of his or her arrival in Montreal. This summit meeting is an important step towards ensuring a top-quality show; not only does it put a human face on a giant event for the performer, but it also allows us the chance to explore and create routines uniquely for the festival. I made a rare exception for Don. Here was a showbiz stalwart who had his stuff down pat and over forty years of experience to back it up. There were no surprises with Don Rickles.

Instead, we ironed out all the details with Tony Oppedisano,[41] Don's road manager and handler. An accomplished singer in his own right, Tony also subbed for Don during the standard afternoon rehearsal. For the first time in my career, a show was ready and rehearsed before I'd met the night's star. Less than an hour before curtain, my cell phone rang. It was Don. Because of the street closures around the theater, his limo driver had gotten lost, and they needed directions. Before he passed me over to the driver, I said, "I look forward to meeting you!" Don's emphatic response was, "Yeah, okay."

---

[41] Better known as Tony O, he was also Frank Sinatra's right-hand man for years, right up to the day Ol' Blue Eyes passed away.

They were only blocks away, so I sent my assistant, Diane Shatz, to the parking lot to greet them. "Make sure you bring him over to me," I instructed. I at least wanted to make his acquaintance before he took to the stage. A few minutes later, Diane tugged at me. "He's coming down the stairs," she said. At this point, it was so close to show time that the backstage corridor was packed with artists, technicians, and assorted hangers-on. I pushed through them all to—finally!—meet Don Rickles. I approached him, hand extended. "Hello, Mr. Rickles. I'm Andy Nulman."

"I don't care," Don cracked—and then he smacked me across the face. The resounding slap caused every head to turn in my direction. I was stunned. I had no idea what to do next. Then Rickles broke through the hush. "Come here, Bubbeleh!" he laughed, wrapping me in a hug. You could feel the relief cascade down the hallway. "I'm just kidding! So nice to meet you . . ." We spent the next five minutes kibbitzing, and we spent three more hours after the show at perhaps the nicest dinner I've ever shared with an artist. Despite his onstage venom, the real-life Rickles is a veritable Mr. Warmth, going far out of his way to remember—and to use—the names of those in his presence.

So how does William Shatner fit into all of this? Well, after I'd stepped down as CEO of Just For Laughs, Bruce Hills asked if I'd stay on as artistic director of the galas for 2000. All the fun without any of the pressure? Let me think about it.

One of the hosts that summer was William Shatner, the Montreal-born actor who went on to achieve fortune and fame as the captain of some sort of starship. It was May, I had to go on a business trip to Los Angeles for my new company anyway, so, keeping with the festival tradition I'd established years earlier, I scheduled an advance meeting with Shatner to discuss his upcoming gala. I sat waiting for him in a Valley coffee shop with my partner Garner Bornstein and Howard Busgang, the former producer of ABC's *Boy Meets World*, who was the head writer for all the Just For Laughs galas. As we waited I told the guys of my fateful meeting with Rickles, and the story was met with much delight. In the middle of the laughter, Shatner walked in. We clammed up, then stood and introduced ourselves.

"Don't let me interrupt you guys," Shatner apologized.

"Naw, it's nothing," I said. "I was just telling them about the time I met Don Rickles."

"Sounded like a good story," said Shatner, sitting down. "Tell me."

What a perfect icebreaker! Sure thing, Bill! In great detail, I recounted yet again my initial encounter with Rickles. The novelty had worn off for Busgang and Bornstein by now, but they gave Shatner a chance to hear the tale. Just as I got to the hug part, Shatner pulled back from the table, cocked his right arm and leveled me with an open-hand drive across the face. (That woke Howard and Garner right up.) Then, with ultimate Captain Kirk staccato pacing, Shatner asked, "What. Am. I. Supposed. To do. Now? Call you. Bubbeleh?" His idea of a joke, I guess. Haw. Haw.

The slap, somewhat heavier than Rickles's love tap, registered 4.3 on the Richter scale. Garner swears it left a white handprint surrounded by pulsating red on my left cheek for fifteen minutes. But what was I supposed to do about it? Sue? Hit him back? Laugh? I shrugged it off and continued with the meeting as if nothing abnormal had happened. I had unique concepts to discuss and gala ideas to sell. Even though I wasn't CEO anymore, Just For Laughs was still in my blood. The blood that was rushing to my left cheek. Once again, I'd taken one for the team. Ow . . .

MAGIC MOMENTS

They weren't all insane. They didn't all strangle, slap, or threaten me. It wasn't always trouble, stress, and brawls. Regardless of the fact that the job was rarely easy, during my fifteen-year tenure helming Just For Laughs, I considered the life I led to be a charmed one. You see, thanks to the festival . . .

. . . I GOT TO DIRECT

You always hear that obnoxious cliché emanating from Hollywood, where eminent thespians announce their true professional desire by uttering, "All I really want to do is direct." But I never really wanted to direct at all; I was merely thrust into the position by our tight economic circumstances.

In 1993, following the success of our tenth-anniversary show, which was chockfull of memory clips from previous years, we decided to re-visit the past once more in our next Showtime show. This time, though, we would request Just For Laughs alumni to provide a taped commentary on their festival experiences. They would be asked, "What does Just For Laughs mean to you?" and their sixty-second answers would, uncharacteristically and unanimously, slam the event, giving the show an unconventional, self-deprecating edge.

I thought the hard part would be lining up the talent, but Paul

Reiser, Bob Newhart, and Mary Tyler Moore fell into place within days (particularly since both Mary and Bob were both managed by the sage Arthur Price, the former president of MTM TV and my mentor since the passing of Marty Klein). Reiser was working on a movie in L.A. at the time, so the production company filmed him and sent us the tape. As for Mary and Bob, both agreed to be filmed in their homes.

I had budgeted about fifteen thousand dollars per shoot, not a ton of money, but enough for camera, lights, sound, and makeup. All we needed then was someone to direct these brief segments. When I looked into the cost of hiring such a person, I almost flipped. To hire a DGA (Directors Guild of America) member to shoot this stuff would've more than doubled the budget. At over sixty thousand dollars, it wasn't worth doing anymore. "No way I'm spending that kind of money to direct a one-minute head shot!" I said. "Christ, even I could do that!"

Suddenly, I realized there was a certain logic to this. Only one problem, though. Other than my kids in family videos, I had never directed anyone in anything before. While I'd be acting in a budgetarily responsible way if I took on this project, I'd also be making my directorial debut working with two of the most illustrious stars in the history of television, TV Hall of Famers both. Uh, where do I sign?

Since there was no *Directing for Dummies* book available back in '93, and since the DGA would murder me if I had the gumption to ask them for lessons, I got a crash course from Patrick Clune, who had directed a number of Just For Laughs episodes in the past. In about forty-five minutes, he gave me the basics, and here's what I learned:

- Make sure there's film in the camera.
- When the tape rolls, ask, "Do we have speed?"—which means, "Is the tape rolling?"
- Once confirmed, wait a beat, then count down, "Three, two, and action!"
- Before saying "action!" stretch out the word "and" as long as you can.
- Don't forget to say "Cut!" when you're done.

Clune's final words of advice to me were, "Hire a good crew and just make sure to look like you know what you're doing at all times. Starting now."

I arrived in New York early for a 10:00 A.M. setup at Mary's palatial Fifth Avenue apartment overlooking Central Park. When Mary hosted our show in 1991, her publicist had described this place as "the Palace of Versailles," and I instantly understood why. Impeccably decorated, filled with tasteful furniture and art, the apartment was as much a museum as it was a home. I prayed I wouldn't break anything.

The shoot would take place in Mary's bedroom, of all places, at 11:00, which gave us an hour to set the lighting and camera position. I described to the cameraman what I wanted (a midshot tightening to a head shot), and waited for America's sweetheart. How cool was this? Starting at the top—directing Mary Tyler Moore in her own bedroom!

At 11:00 precisely, Mary entered her boudoir, met the crew, and, after exchanging niceties with everyone, assumed her position—leaning against the antique writing desk in the corner. Mary and I had worked together in '91, but under different circumstances; I was a mere executive producer back then. Would she actually listen to me as a director? Time to find out.

Here's what we were shooting that day. Mary would be asked the "What does it mean to you?" question, to which she would reply, in her typical effervescent manner: "Wonderful! Being surrounded by so many funny people from all over—I mean, the spirit was magic, it was just wonderful!" She would continue to enthuse like this, smiling all the way. "Obviously, working with Billy, Robin, and Whoopi was a thrill for me. I admire them so much. And then, of course, knowing that what we were doing, we were doing for the homeless, well, it just made me feel so good inside!"

At that point Mary would be interrupted by a voice. As the camera framed her in a close-up, the voice would point out her mistake. No, we're not talking about Comic Relief here; we're talking about Just For Laughs, in Montreal. Mary's joy would rapidly disintegrate into disgust. "Oh, yeah . . . Montreal." She would shudder, not knowing what to say for a moment, and then recall the festival's mascot: "Uh, I remember that ugly green thing!" And that would be it. Granted, it was no *Apocalypse Now*, but to me it was a start.

After setting up the situation and confirming that we had "speed," I recited the magic words. "Aaaaaaannnnnnnnnnnnnnnnnd . . . action!" Amazing! Mary Tyler Moore actually listened! Cut! Let's do this again. But this time with additional motivation. "For this take, Mary, when you say 'so good inside,' I want you to give yourself a little hug," I encouraged. "Aaaaaaannnnnnnnnnnnnnnnnd . . . action!" And so it went, for about fifteen takes. I was getting into this big time. With each successive take, I added another miniscule subtlety—close your eyes on the shudder, sneer on the word "Montreal"—nudging her performance to new heights. "You can do it, Mare," I cheer-led each time.

"For the next one," I began at one point—but I was quickly cut off. "No, Andy, there are no next ones," Mary said firmly, but she was still smiling. "I think we got what you need." The queen had spoken.

"I could get used to this," I said to myself after viewing the tape. One take was barely discernible from the next, but I studied them all like they were the Dead Sea Scrolls. I was a director now, and I wanted to make sure that we used the very best material. I was so into this that by the time I got to Newhart's house I was wearing jodhpurs and carrying a riding crop.

In later years, I directed a huge, outdoor stage show and, in Just For Laughs galas, directed stars like Kevin James, Rob Lowe, Nathan Lane, and Tim Allen (as the first male to do *The Vagina Monologues*). But none of this would have been possible without Mary Tyler Moore. She was a true confidence-builder, playing the game with the neophyte who wanted to be Cecil B. DeMille that day in her bedroom.

. . . I GOT TO MEET MY BOYHOOD HEROES

As a kid, I was a sports and music enthusiast, but my real heroes were the people who made cartoons. While I loved the onscreen lunacy, I was more intrigued by the guys behind the scenes, the demented personalities who thought up and delivered it. In 1988 I read a fascinating article in the *Los Angeles Times* about a retrospective honoring the animation work of one of my favorites, Jay Ward. The wacky creator of Rocky and Bullwinkle, Dudley Do-Right, George of the Jungle, and other "too hip for the room" cartoon characters was renowned for being far more eccentric than the whimsical life forms he invented for TV. The *Times* article exposed much of his abnormality, describing, for example, the time he sent a mannequin fitted with a tape recorder to be a stand-in at his daughter's wedding.

I gave Bruce Hills the mission of bringing the Jay Ward retrospective to Just For Laughs in 1989. Our timing, once again, was ideal. During the '88 festival I had put together an intimate exhibition of original cartoon artwork with Mort Walker's Museum of Cartoon Art,[42] and the response it received was all the official justification I needed to pursue other such non-stand-up comedy projects. Unofficially, though, I just wanted to realize a childhood fantasy by working with Jay Ward's stuff. After hundreds of phone calls, months of negotiation, and some impressive detective work, Bruce finalized an arrangement with Billie Ward, Jay's wife. We were to solidify the deal during a trip to L.A. in June. I was ecstatic.

On June 9, Bruce and I showed up at Dudley Do-Right's Emporium, a bungalow-style souvenir shop located directly across the street from the Chateau Marmont Hotel[43] on Sunset Boulevard. The antithesis of Disney corporate slick, this homespun homestead, with its plaster figures of Rocky and Bullwinkle twirling on the roof, sold sweatshirts, watches, and other licensed products from Jay Ward's menagerie. Billie signed the contract, sold me a hand-painted cel (a single plastic sheet used in creating traditional animation) of my favorite moose, and nonchalantly asked, "Do you want to meet Jay?"

I was astonished, for this was a truly unexpected dream come true. Ward was a notorious recluse; he'd even refused to be interviewed for the *Times* article, so why would he consent to see us? It had to be a hoax of some sort. Bruce, however, had a different reaction to the invitation. "Oh, the poor, delusional woman," he whispered to me as we went behind the Do-Right Emporium to a second, hidden bungalow. "Humor her and go along with it." For some strange reason, Bruce thought Jay was dead. Billie led us into the house, and there we

---

[42] Walker was the creator of the Beetle Bailey and Hi and Lois comic strips.

[43] Gossip-loving readers may recognize the name of this Hollywood landmark as the place where John Belushi overdosed and died.

My all-time favorite festival photo. I direct, and Tim Allen actually listens.

PHOTO BY SHANE KELLEY

glimpsed a dazzling pipe organ, a rolltop desk, and giant, gilt-edged original movie posters of classics like *Mighty Joe Young*. She called out, "Jay, I brought you Andy and Bruce!" and left. We sat and waited—Bruce for a ghost, me for an enigma or a letdown.

Thirty seconds later, he entered the room. I knew he was the real thing—I had seen pictures of Jay Ward, and here was the same face, although slightly older. We chatted for about half an hour about animation, the origins of characters (particularly the Mountie Dudley), and zillions of other topics I brought up in my crazed-fan state. Why he chose to talk to us I still don't know, but I could've gone on for hours. Unfortunately, reality reared its ugly head. There was business at hand. Time to get down to it.

Jay wasn't coming to the festival himself (June Foray, the voice of Rocky the Flying Squirrel, Natasha, and hundreds of other cartoon characters, was to be our guest for the special event), but we needed his help selecting the optimal mix of cartoons to be screened. After we'd arrived at a consensus on titles, I asked Jay when we could get a broker to start working on the arduous process of procuring and shipping the film cans. "Oh forget that," he laughed. "Let me just give 'em to you now." And, with that, Jay Ward shuffled back and forth from another room, eventually piling twenty flat, grey cans into two boxes at our feet. "I don't know," I hesitated. "Isn't there an industry standard as per shipping film?" Jay simply replied, "Just stuff 'em in your suitcases."

So we did, clanking through customs, each smuggling ten cans of film layered between our underwear, socks, and T-shirts. I still don't know the extent of the "illegality" of what we did, but, as an insurance policy, I had asked Jay if he could write a note describing the contents of the cans. He pulled out a pad of pink paper, which was personalized with the heading "A Memo From Jay Ward Productions Inc.," and wrote, by hand:

June 9th, 1989
VIEWING PURPOSES ONLY!
NOT PORNOGRAPHIC,
NOT IMMORAL
AND
NOT INDECENT!

This signed memo is one of my most cherished mementos, and it hangs on the wall in my study just above the iMac I'm using to write this book. To its immediate right is something just as (if not more) rare and cherished. It's a pencil drawing of Michigan J. Frog, the hot-and-cold star of the Chuck Jones classic *One Froggy Evening*,[44] signed by Chuck Jones himself.

The Jay Ward event went so well that I decided to shoot for the moon the next year and go after Jones, my all-time idol. Chuck conceived cartoon characters like The Roadrunner and Wile E. Coyote; and,

---

[44] In 1991 this cartoon was voted Top Hollywood Cartoon of All Time at Just For Laughs by a blue-ribbon panel that included Steven Spielberg, Martin Scorsese, Joe Dante, and *Time* magazine film critic Jay Cocks.

while he didn't create Bugs Bunny, it was his madcap vision that defined the wascally wabbit's enduring personality. In my mind, his masterful Puccini parody *The Rabbit of Seville* is one of the finest bits of comedy anywhere, ever. Through his daughter Linda and Steven Paul Leiva, the head of Chuck Jones Productions at the time, we brought Chuck to town for a special tribute held at the ornate Rialto Cinema on July 13 and 14, 1990.

A mischievous Colonel Sanders look-alike, Chuck was a feisty little leprechaun. He was also a consummate flirt, and he tirelessly wooed the makeup and hair women we'd hired to touch him up for a segment we were inserting into our Showtime show. At a dinner following the Friday night première, Chuck scolded Leiva for interrupting a conversation he was having with Tanis Gravenor, a blond bombshell who worked in our PR department. "Steve," he said firmly, "the more you want to talk about business, the less time I'll have to talk to Tanis!"

During the Showtime shoot, Chuck charmed the pants off grizzled TV vets like Bob Kaminsky and Paul Miller, both of whom lined up for autographed sketches when the cameras stopped rolling. But perhaps the defining Chuck Jones moment was his exit from the stage on opening night.

Built in 1924 and fashioned on the Opéra de Paris, the Rialto was one of those old-fashioned movie houses with a screen positioned approximately seven feet off the ground and two feet from the lip of the stage. We had brought a podium onstage for Chuck to speak and answer questions from before the screening of his work. When he was done, he would descend a steep, narrow, rickety staircase to his front-row seat. Jones was nearly eighty. He used a cane, and we were petrified that he would take a tumble. Leiva suggested that we get two women to help him down the stairs, but Chuck wouldn't hear of it (go figure, even though one of them was Tanis).

On June 13 the crowd went nuts when Chuck concluded by saying, "So, let's watch some cartoons!" Leiva and I held our breath as he approached the steps. He took one step, then another, and then . . . he started to waver. His body contorted one way, then the other. Leiva and I held each other's breath. The crowd gasped. Then, with a roguish grin, Chuck righted himself, stood perfectly erect, skipped down three steps, leapt off the staircase, and executed a perfect three-point landing on the floor—to yet another ovation.

The following year we held our third animation retrospective at the Rialto, this time featuring Joseph Barbera, of Hanna-Barbera fame (The Flintstones, The Jetsons, Huckleberry Hound, among countless other creations). While the concept continued to be popular—tickets sold out within days—I decided to drop it after 1991. I wanted to quit while I was ahead. And after I had exhausted my list of major boyhood idols.

. . . I GOT TO WITNESS THE BIRTH OF MR. BEAN

By the late 1990s Rowan Atkinson had accomplished something the world hadn't seen since the days of Charlie Chaplin. As the nonverbal Mr. Bean, he had become a global comedy star, his massive appeal unhampered by political borders and language barriers.[45] I look upon his success with a sense of paternal pride, as the seed that eventually gave birth to Mr. Bean was planted on the stages of Just For Laughs.

Rowan made his festival debut in 1987, and Gilbert and I immediately became great friends with him and his new manager, Rowan's old school buddy Peter Bennett-Jones. In 1989 Peter approached us with an intriguing offer. Rowan would return to the festival and be part of our HBO telecast, provided that we give him some stage time . . . during a French gala. Had I heard right? A *French* gala? Peter explained Rowan's motivation in a letter (pre-e-mail, kids!) dated June 13: "This is primarily because he will not be known to any of the French-speaking audiences, and, as you know, the principal purpose of his performing the material to non-English audiences who don't know who the Dickens he is, is to test their reaction as part of our research into response to his mime work."

So, with very little fanfare, Rowan—with colleague Angus Deayton—performed a couple of short pieces of "mime work," as Peter put it, in our French galas. The audience loved every second of it and howled

---

[45] I heard a great story about Rowan's attitude towards fame. He was so in love with France that he didn't let his manager sell his *Mr. Bean* show in that country; he wanted there to be at least one place in the world he could go without being hounded by fans asking him to make a funny face or to take a pratfall.

their approval at the end of the performance. We sent Peter a tape of Rowan's act at the end of the '89 festival, and he used it as his Mr. Bean demo for Thames Television and BBC in the U.K. The British networks bit hard, and *Mr. Bean,* the TV show, was launched soon afterwards.

Unfortunately—foolishly, perhaps—that's about as far as our involvement with Rowan's project went (and we had our fingers in the pie as early as April, when we tried to drum up North American broadcast interest in what was then being described by Peter as, "an initial series of three short, silent films featuring Rowan"). But, to this day, every time I catch *Mr. Bean* on TV or in a plane cabin filled with laughter (it's the most popular piece of in-flight programming in the world), I smile at the knowledge that I was there for this most immaculate of conceptions.

. . . I GOT TO LAUGH MYSELF SILLY

Oh, the laughter. As the sappy Streisand song goes, it's what I'll remember. At Just For Laughs we laughed at everything. At good things, at bad things, at each other. We laughed at genius, at stupidity, at sophistication, at vulgarity. One way we got through the never-ending hard times was by chanting, "One day, we'll look back on this and laugh." We were never wrong.

Of all the laughter, though, there is one particular story that never fails to set me a-giggling. Like foolish grade-school boys, Bruce, Willie, and I still kill ourselves over "Cathy Ladman's Phantom Joke." Here's the story.

In 1996 Cathy Ladman made her festival debut. While not the strongest member of the female comic brigade, this staff writer for Roseanne was competent, a truly nice woman, and, after so many years of auditioning, deserving of a festival shot. That year we booked Cathy to perform in a number of Just For Laughs shows, but the main reason for her visit was the televised gala set. Do well at this, and, at best, you'll get your own TV show; at worst, you'll wind up with a great demo tape (and look what that did for Rowan Atkinson!).

Unfortunately, Cathy didn't have a good night at the gala. When we reviewed the tape, we were saddened by the silence that greeted most of her material. You could tell, as well, by looking at her face, that she was disappointed by the crowd's reaction to her. Yet, ever the warrior, she carried on, delivering her jokes to the void. Then, an unexpected sound disrupted the silence, ever so slightly.

Somebody broke wind.

The muffled fart caused ripples of laughter to cascade through the theater. Hearing these minor laugh waves, Cathy's face instantaneously brightened. Unaware of the fart, Cathy thought the audience amusement was in response to the tepid line she had just delivered. Thus, she delivered her next line with more gusto. A bit more laughter.

It's too bad that Cathy was near the end of her set. Had she come onstage a little later, perhaps the passed gas would have pushed her routine to a higher level. Still, the bum rumble was the turning point, and, just thinking about that magic moment—that instant between fart, chuckles, and the Ladman lift—remains a catalyst for cracking me up to this very day.

. . . I GOT TO SING

Writing, directing, producing is a blast, but it's work. Actually being part of the show is magic; the memory stays with you forever.

My singing debut at Just For Laughs came in 1990, when the late Bill Hicks, a brilliant and caustic comedian, decided to form a de facto festival band to perform at the closing party. Hicks himself was an impressive guitarist, and he asked me to help recruit other musicians for his ensemble from the Just For Laughs guest list. A few days later the band was complete: Hicks on lead guitar, MTV's Don Jamieson on bass, willow-haired publicist Michael O'Brien on drums, and me on the microphone.

I sing about as well as I play goalie; I'm not very good, but I'm stupid enough to get out there and face the music. On the Sunday night of the party, either our entire audience was drunk or we experienced one of those brief moments in life when everything comes together as you actually plan it. Whichever it was, our rendition of The Troggs's "Wild Thing" was met with wild applause. That was it for set number one. Buoyed by the response, we actually went out again about ninety minutes later to perform a brutal version of Led Zeppelin's "Rock and Roll." We should have quit while we were ahead. It was so bad I vowed never to sing in public again.

My self-imposed ban held for ten years, but, in 2000, as the director of the festival's galas I was once again thrust behind a voice-amplification device. This time I would lead a chorus of Mounties (there's that costume again!) backing up gala host Eric Idle as he sang Monty Python's timeless "Lumberjack Song." I didn't require much arm twisting. I'd always been a huge Python fan, and Eric was an extreme pro and a pleasure to work with. As one of the few people around who knew all the words to the song, my job was to assemble the choir and teach the number to them.

The St. Denis Theater audience was larger and substantially more sober than the party animals we'd serenaded in 1990, but they seemed to enjoy the performance even more than I did. In fact, the first beaming face I noticed in the crowd when leading the Mountie march onstage was that of Bob Milton, the usually dead-serious president of Air Canada. For me, one of the highlights of the night was running into him after the show. "I envy you," Bob confided quietly. "Singing 'The Lumberjack Song' with the guy from Monty Python? That was always a dream of mine. But singing onstage as a Mountie . . . somehow, I don't think the shareholders would appreciate that."

. . . I GOT TO WORK WITH SOME MIGHTY CLASS ACTS

There were many, so many, who stood out—but, hey, I have to save some material for the sequel to this book. Here's one I think you'll appreciate.

When Jim Carrey came to Just For Laughs in 1990 he was a phenomenal entertainer about to catch his second wind. His first go-round in Hollywood was marked by a failed sitcom (NBC's *Duck Factory*) and a vampire movie with Lauren Hutton that didn't fare much better. Now, after years in limbo, he was working his way back with standout performances in *Earth Girls Are Easy* and Fox's *In Living Color* (in which he played the token white guy). We paid Carrey two thousand dollars for a week's work, and he was happy to take it (these days, of course, a blink of his eye will cost you more than two grand). He was respectful, modest, and gentlemanly. One of my great memories is of the closing gala, when Jim stood next to another up-and-comer during the curtain call: Tim Allen.

People who saw Jim's gala set still marvel at his elastic body, his vocal range, and the mind-altering variety of his material (from Jimmy Stewart's reaction to a nuclear holocaust to an Iranian Top 40 radio tribute). What's more, many of the famous Carrey lines that we would hear later, in his films ("Al-righty, then!" among others), surfaced in his stage routine. I've said many times that the world may have gained a movie star, but it also lost a supreme live talent in the process.

A couple of years later—after working with legends like Bob Newhart and Mary Tyler Moore—we were looking for a younger, hipper host for our Showtime show, and I thought of Carrey. I spoke to his managers, and they actually pressed me to sign him, saying how perfect Jim would be for the spot, especially considering that his hot new film was being released soon. I called Jay Larkin at Showtime and pitched the idea. "We did a Jim Carrey special, and it didn't do well for us at all," he said, coldly dismissing the idea. "Besides, don't believe all the hype you hear. Every comedian and his mother are starring in a 'hot new film.'" The film turned out to be *Ace Ventura, Pet Detective*.

While Jim Carrey never again played Just For Laughs, our paths crossed once more, in the fall of 1997. His manager, Jimmy Miller, had heard about the security detail I had put together for Roseanne that summer and called to ask if I could arrange the same for Jim, who was coming to Montreal to spend a weekend with his buddy Nicolas Cage (in town to film the thriller *Snake Eyes*). Jim also wanted to see the Canadiens-Bruins hockey game at the Molson Center, so I put together a whole package of info and tickets to drop off for him at the Ritz-Carlton Hotel.

Hearing of this errand, my sons, Aidan and Hayes, went absolutely berserk. Jim Carrey was their number-one fave, so they sat right down and wrote him a letter, begging him to autograph the *Disney Adventure* magazines (with you-know-who on the cover) that they wanted to include in the package I'd prepared. On the condition that they swore not to leak the news to their friends, I promised to take them over to the Ritz to drop off their stuff in person.

I didn't expect much in return, and I prepared my kids for the very distinct possibility that they'd get no response. "Guys, he's a big star and very, very busy," I explained. As a firm believer in M. Scott Peck's theory, "Expect the bad and be surprised at the good," I wanted to soften the blow if it had to be delivered.

Over a week went by, and nothing. My kids went from being acutely disappointed to forgetting all about it. Then, late one Monday night, the phone rang at the Nulman household. I was out playing hockey, and my wife answered.

"Can I speak to Andy, please?"

"He's out playing hockey. Who's calling?"

"Hi, it's Jim Carrey. Is this Mrs. Nulman?"

"Yes, why?"

"Your kids sent me this delightful letter, and I autographed all their magazines, but there was no return address, so I'm calling to find out how to get this to you."

Two days later a FedEx package arrived at my office. In it was a handwritten reply to my kids from Jim, plus a half-dozen magazines. Class act. Yet another keepsake on the charm bracelet of my festival life.

HOW I ALMOST KILLED GEORGE BURNS

You waited this long, so I might as well tell you . . .

From the minute I booked George Burns for the 1993 festival, I became strangely preoccupied with the idea of his death. He was ninety-seven at the time, and even though his publicity stills (which had to have been shot at least a decade earlier) depicted him as a blithe old sprite perched upon a vaudeville trunk, I knew that he was more frail than the public had been led to believe. A lot more frail.

You see, about a month earlier I had met George Burns at his manager's office in Los Angeles. Sweet and pleasant, he sat in a corner on an elevated director's chair, scanning *Daily Variety* and puffing on his omnipresent trademark cigar. Somewhat less sweet was manager Irving Fein, who spent his time smoking me, instead. One hundred thousand dollars and a cashmere sweater later,[46] it was all Fein and dandy: Burns was signed. North America's most legendary funnyman would come to Montreal and perform a full concert at Place des Arts on Sunday, appear in the Saturday night gala at the St. Denis Theater (which would be taped for our Showtime TV special), and be inducted into the Just For Laughs Museum's Humor Hall of Fame on Saturday

---

[46] Judy Pastore, who was head of Showtime's comedy programs at the time, advised me that the way to Irving Fein's heart was via cashmere, hence the odd currency.

afternoon. That's a lot of work for anyone to do in two days, let alone a fragile ninety-seven year old.

Because we were a bunch of cynical showbiz degenerates at Just For Laughs, Burns's mortality became the running joke around the office as soon as I broke the news. You couldn't bring the man's name up to anyone at any time without being met with, "You think he's gonna make it here?" The jokes were so pervasive that I wouldn't have been surprised to discover some sort of backroom betting pool (remember the infamous Milton Berle incident?) based on the date and time of Burns's prefestival demise.

Burns had signed contracts for two one-hundredth-birthday-celebration concerts: one at the Palladium in London on his actual birth-date, January 20, 1996; the other at Caesar's Palace in Las Vegas shortly thereafter. The whole world wanted to see George Burns make it to that mystical, miraculous century mark. I just wanted to see him make it to Montreal in July.

I'm sure you've all had those days when some song runs through your head like a recurring soundtrack—a pesky tune you can't get rid of, no matter how hard you try. Right about this time, mine was a little ditty first performed at Just For Laughs back in 1985 by the Canadian duo of Al and George. Primarily song parodists (their version of David Lee Roth's "I'm Just a Gigolo" was called "I'm Just a Big Asshole"), the duo highlighted their '85 set with an original melody called—are you ready for this?—"Hurry Up and Die George Burns." Try as I might to exorcise it, Al and George's apocalyptic tune reverberated through my medulla oblongata from the moment I shook hands with Irving Fein on the deal. (For months I worried every time the phone rang that Fein had somehow stumbled upon the song and was calling to cancel. Worse yet, to sue.)

Death. Death. Death. I was obsessed. I saw visions of The Grim Reaper in my cereal bowl. Funeral processions seemed to cross every intersection I stopped at. My anxiety increased when I received the signed copy of the contract. One ominous clause had been added in Fein's handwriting: "If, for whatever reason, *Artist* cannot perform the contracted obligations, all monies will be immediately refunded to *Festival*."

True, it's a relatively standard clause—at least, standard for you and me. But for a ninety-seven year old it could only mean one thing: he's gonna go before he gets here. Or, worse than that, he's gonna go *when* he gets here! Or, worse still, he's gonna go when he gets here, and *I'll* be held responsible! Paranoid? Maybe so, but that worst-case scenario almost came to pass during the nearly tragic Hall of Fame induction ceremony that sunny Saturday afternoon. (At this point, I urge the squeamish to close the book—it's all over for you now.)

The night before, Burns had wowed a packed theater with an "un-scheduled" walk-on during a gala show hosted by John Candy. He told a few jokes and sang "Gracie," an ode to his late wife and former part-ner, Gracie Allen.[47] This was the first time I had ever seen George Burns live onstage, and I was overwhelmed by the metamorphosis I witnessed. Just seconds before, waiting backstage, he'd been an old man in a shiny tux. Yet, as soon as the first beams of stage light touched his skin, a transformation had taken place. Like a luminous fountain of youth, the lights bathed him with vigor; the years seemed to fall from him in waves.

The crowd went nuts when he finished, and he capped off the magic with a classic Burnsian move: upon being presented with a tro-phy by an adorable festival hostess, he said to Candy, "Here, you keep the award. I'll take the kid." And he walked off with her, arm-in-arm, back into the shadows.

Okay . . . back to the harsh reality of Saturday afternoon.

After all of this, I finally managed to erase the images of Burns's premature death from my mind. Al and George's song was relegated to the oldies bin, and I was calm, cool, and contented as I waited for Burns, Fein, et al. to arrive for the induction ceremony.

To fully comprehend the Kennedy assassination, you have to understand the physical layout of Dealey Plaza and the Texas School-book Depository; to fully comprehend the near-tragic George Burns

---

[47] Actually, he had to sing it twice. The first time, he and his piano player—a seventy-five year old that Burns and the octogenarian Fein called "Kid"—were so out of sync that you'd swear they were performing two different songs. Director Paul Miller stopped the show, which was rolling live to tape as a safety net for the TV broadcast. After a short delay Burns reappeared as if the first take had never happened and nailed it. The audience was so enraptured by him that they would've sat through one hundred more.

George Burns: a sprite in his official publicity photo.
When bathed in stage lights, years fell off him in waves.

Hall of Fame induction ceremony, you have to understand the physical layout of the Just For Laughs Museum. The ceremony was to take place in the middle of a deep atrium. A dais was set up, and on it was placed a table where Burns and Fein could hold court. I would be off to the side with a microphone, ready to moderate questions from the swarm of media that would occupy the floor space in front of the stage.[48] Media and guests would also fill the three tiers of balconies that surrounded and looked down on the dais. And, high overhead, scraping the tippy-top of the atrium, fifty feet above Burns-level, one story above the last guest, were a half-dozen confetti throwers. But more on them later.

The gathered media types were buzzing—many of them had witnessed the Burns enchantment the night before. Come to think of it, virtually everyone lucky enough to be there that Saturday afternoon knew they were in for something rare and exceptional: a private audience with George Burns! The showbiz icon! One of the most beloved superstars of all time! The living legend who was—Yes! Yes!—still living!

George Christy, the longtime *Hollywood Reporter* social columnist, had requested a picture of yours truly and Burns for his popular feature The Great Life, and I had told his photographer that we'd do it as soon as Burns arrived. The moment had come. I was beckoned backstage, and there was Burns. In a wheelchair! "Don't worry," Fein assured me. "This is how we get him around to avoid tiring him out." Logical, yes, but still unsettling. "Just make sure nobody sees him like this."

The photo was taken with me bending down and leaning in as close as possible to hide the wheelchair handles. I smiled—beamed, actually—all the while harboring doubts as to whether the museum lights would have the same effect as those at the theater. Three minutes later it was time to find out. Flanked by two blonde babes to play up our honored guest's randy stereotype, I stepped up to the Plexiglas

---

[48] "Swarm" was indeed the operative word. I drove our publicists crazy in my attempt to make sure that everyone who owned as much as an eight-millimeter camera showed up for this one. In the end, all four American TV networks and the two major Canadian networks were joined by scores of French-language and European camera crews. On the print side, everyone from Associated Press to the *New York Times* to the *Canadian Jewish News* was there, snapping photos and filing stories. It was our biggest media turnout ever.

podium. "Ladies and gentlemen," I boomed into the mike, "George Burns." Eruption.

The curtain, which moments earlier had concealed a wheelchair, opened to reveal Fein and Burns, smiling and erect (well, standing, at least). *Phew!* The conference turned out to be an even better show than the previous night's performance had been. Sure, Burns's answers were stock (Question: "How come you go out with younger women?" Answer: "I can't find any my age."), but the man's charm was irresistible. He answered questions posed by men, but he worked the questions posed by women into a good-natured, flirtatious dialogue, turning each successive response a female reporter would give into yet another setup line.

After about twenty-five minutes of this banter, it was time for the official induction ceremony. Music, mood lighting, and the announcement, "The Just For Laughs Humor Hall of Fame is proud to induct . . . George Burns!"

Remember those confetti throwers I referred to earlier? Well, at the mention of Burns's name they were supposed to toss out handfuls of celebratory confetti. But not just any confetti. This was *big* confetti. *Real* big confetti. About the size of dollar bills. Each one printed with the museum's logo on one side and "Congratulations, George Burns" (and a head shot of the star) on the other.

Now, the confetti was bundled together in packs of about 250. Each pack had the look, the consistency, and the density of a common household brick. Each pack was secured by two rubber bands, one at either end. All the confetti throwers had to do was remove a rubber band from one end, toss the bundle into the air, and the laws of physics would do the rest; air pressure would spread the bills and pop off the remaining rubber band. The end result would be like a storm of giant-sized snowflakes.

And, for the most part, it was. Except that one confetti thrower forgot to remove one rubber band from one brick. Remember the "He's gonna go when he gets here, and *I'll* be held responsible!" nightmare scenario I mentioned earlier? Well, here it was. Now.

Picture this: Paper snowstorm. Wild cheering. Music blaring. Fein,

George Burns accepts his Humor Hall of Fame Award from me,
blissfully unaware of the near-tragedy that lies ahead for both of us.

resplendent in a new cashmere sweater, beaming with pride. And a brick of big confetti, tightly bound by two elastics, descending rapidly, on a collision course with the delicate cranium of an unsuspecting ninety-seven-year-old man.

What made me look up and see this hurtling brick in the midst of everything else that was going on, I still don't know. Perhaps it was the sound. Think back, if you will, to those classic Roadrunner cartoons. Remember the sound Wile E. Coyote made as he plummeted off a mountain peak into a dusty canyon? Well, that's the sound that a confetti brick makes as it plunges downward through four stories of atrium. It's a weird, raspy, whistling sound, one that intensifies as the brick continues its nosedive.

At this moment I learned a lot about life. I learned how fast one's mind can work, for in the time it took that bundle to travel halfway to its final destination, the following images ran through my brain:

- George Burns's skull crushed like Humpty Dumpty.
- Four dozen TV and newspaper cameras capturing the gruesome sight live.[49]
- The unsettling story leading off every newscast in the Western World.
- Standing in line at the unemployment office after the festival goes bankrupt.
- Being stigmatized for the rest of my life as "the guy who killed George Burns."

I also learned that at a time like this your legs and arms and mouth work at a speed inversely proportionate to that of your mind. As, seemingly, the only witness to the upcoming carnage, I tried to dive, jump—anything!—but my feet were riveted to the museum's cement floor. I tried to cry out a warning, but instead I spewed consonants and verbs at random, sounding something like, "Ughheowahhh!"

I watched it unfold like a bad spaghetti western, all in slow motion. The crowd's frantic applause became labored. The wild lights now tracked smoothly across the atrium like skyscraper beacons. And the brick continued towards its date with destiny.

Bang!

When the brick finally touched down, it hit the table where Burns was seated, missing his toupee by about an inch and a half. The resounding crack startled Burns and Fein for a second, but, because of all the ruckus, nobody else even noticed. The brick bounced off the table and landed behind the stage, out of sight and out of harm's way. Fein never even mentioned it, but he winked strangely as he passed me on his way out. *Phew, again!*

Luckily, Burns had been leaning back at the moment of impact. If he'd been leaning forward, as he was just moments earlier while answering questions, perhaps this story would have had a different, more tragic ending. Let's just say that, like baseball, comedy is a game of inches.

---

[49] Suddenly, my "Get 'em all there at all costs" media initiative didn't seem like the best of strategies.

And when Burns did eventually pass away, in 1996—of natural causes, thankfully—I couldn't help but smile. Not the smile you smile when you're happy, mind you; the smile you smile when you dodge a bullet. Because, in this case, George Burns and I both dodged a big one. He had made it to one hundred. And I had made it to the next festival. Unstigmatized.

THE CEO BASKS

The FedEx guy was late. It wasn't his fault, though. The rugged, truck-driving emissary was battling the last winter storm of the season, making Saturday shipments to weekend customers too impatient to wait for normal business hours to resume on Monday morning. Although there were dozens of other packages he had to deliver that day, none was more important than the holy grail I awaited with bated—and frozen—breath: the envelope stuffed with the final galleys of this book.

Despite its importance, the envelope didn't look like much when I finally got my grubby hands on it—a nondescript pouch with some waybills slipped into a plastic pocket. But, after I'd spent a year laboring to describe fifteen years of my labor, it served to bring closure to the most exciting time of my life. I pulled up a chair and sat down to read my words.

The book's concept was simple: I'd retrace my comedy career and the steps that brought me there. I figured that the sentimental part would be writing it, and, aside from the ego boost I'd get when I came across the volume in bookstores, my emotional attachment to it would be minimal once it was completed. Yet here I was, on this snowy Saturday, enraptured by my own story. Wow, did I actually live all this?

Yet another magic moment is born.

Unfortunately, the moment was experiencing labor pains. We had a Bar Mitzvah to attend that night, and it was now just an hour prior to the scheduled start time. My wife, Lynn, was busy upstairs attending to the needs of our two sons; Aidan's hair wasn't working out and Hayes's suit was stained. Their three-way screaming played out as a loud, surly symphony.

And where was I during this calamity? Unshaven, dressed in tattered jeans and a sweatshirt, I calmly sipped coffee at my dining room table, drowning in a backwash of nostalgia. But Lynn was in a state of panic. Despite her best efforts, yet another family outing was getting off to a late start. "Andy," she hyperventilated. "You've got to get ready! My God, you haven't even showered!"

Yet, oblivious to this spousal stimulus, I carried on reading. While finishing up the legend of how Chris Lynam's butt stole the show during his 1990 festival appearance, I felt the unceremonious plunk of my tuxedo pants thrown from the hallway to my right. Ouch. I got the hint. I also got upstairs, fast.

And as the opening jolts of water beat on the bathtub floor, as I gathered shampoo and soap, as Lynn washed out Hayes's stain and deftly fixed Aidan's skewed tresses, I strode off into the shower's wetness, thinking, with a smile: "You know, one day someone oughtta make a movie about all this stuff!"

Over and above the 15-year career that gave him the credentials to write this book, Andy Nulman is an accomplished public speaker, an award-winning TV producer, an inventive stage show director, an avid snowboarder, a fearless hockey goalie, a voracious reader, a pop music connoisseur and a chic fashion plate. Acclaimed as a "Top 40 Under 40" business leader by *The Financial Post*, Andy is currently the president of Airborne Entertainment, a pioneer in the world of wireless media. This is his third book . . . and hopefully, not his last.